I have been blown away reading Cody's insights on the familiar stories of Jesus' encounters with women in the Gospels. I thought I had thoroughly considered each story, but through these devotionals I am drawn deeper into the wonder of what it means to engage with Jesus. Carve out some time to savor each one. You will be blessed!

-Kathy Phillips, Bible teacher and founder of
Prepare for Life Bible Study

Cody is a trusted guide for anyone looking to find Jesus. With her unique gift to engage both your mind and your heart she will have you seeing the Living Christ in ways you've never considered before. There is no doubt *Jesus By Her Side* will make a tremendous difference in your life.

-Curtis Jones, Network Director at *Convoy of Hope*

Cody writes with the words as one who has sat long at the feet of Jesus. Like Mary, she has chosen the one thing that is necessary (Luke 10:42) and invites us, as women, to choose and encounter Him as well. Cody is a guide you can trust to help you see Jesus with fresh eyes and renewed courage and faith.

-Susannah Baker, author of *Restore: Remembering Life's Hurts with the God Who Rebuilds* and founder of
Restore Ministries for Women

As we read the Gospels, it's often easy to overlook how intentional Jesus was in his interactions with women. In *Jesus By Her Side*, Cody invites us to learn how these relationships can inform the way we view Jesus beside us in our daily living. These poignant devotionals provide a timely reminder that indeed "Jesus Christ is the same yesterday, today and forever" (Heb. 13:8).

-Courtney Garrett, Bible teacher and author of *101: Exploring the Basics of the Christian Faith*

This book is deep, witty, profound, and entertaining. Cody's deep knowledge of women in the Bible is evident throughout these pages. The way she relates the history of these important women of the Bible to the lives we live as women now is stunning and so relatable. You will not want to put this down as her honesty and boldness is wrapped in comfort and softness and her words will lead you directly to the heart and feet of Jesus. Having the opportunity to learn about God's heart for us through the women in the Bible in a way that is understandable, enjoyable, and attention-keeping is just what we all need.

-Meredyth Fletcher, Holistic Nutritionist and Biblical Counselor, Founder of *Karpos Wellness*

It is my sincere pleasure to know and love Cody Andras. By God's divine design, I met Cody while she and her family toured Israel where our hearts deeply connected for God's people and kingdom advancement! Cody is an insightful, intelligent and worshipful woman of God who graciously communicates God's Word with authority and anointing. Her devotions causes you to grow in faith and examine your heart for areas the Lord desires to touch! All glory to God for Cody using her gifts to advance His kingdom!

-Chrissie Shaheen, Founder, Executive Director and Missionary of *The Tent Ministries*

This book is a timely invitation to every woman who longs to know the Jesus from Scripture in a very personal way. Cody's writing style succeeds in making these Gospel accounts come alive and it presents Jesus' powerful and timeless invitation to every longing heart. This is a must-read, but even more than that, this book will inevitably offer us the opportunity to respond to the One who longs for us to encounter Him in our everyday moments.

-Corlischa Badenhorst, Women's minister in Houston, TX

For the past two years, we have gathered as a small group in Cody's living room to seek Jesus not only beside one another, but confident of His presence beside us and among us as well. The prayer exercises Cody writes in the chapters of her book are exercises we continue to practice in our weekly small group. There is no doubt you will meet with Jesus between the pages of this book, whether you read it alone or with others.

-Lindsee Eddy, Houston, TX

Cody Andras's words are guideposts that help us navigate the day-to-day mess of life and beckon us into the presence of God. Please read this book. Her words invite us into a deeper look into the stories in the Scriptures that wrap us in the tenderness and compassionate arms of Christ.

-Natalie Mott, Houston, TX

Jesus
by
her side

Jesus by her side

Finding the Nearness of God Through the Eyes of the Women in the Gospels

cody andras

Jesus By Her Side
Copyright© 2023 by Cody Andras

Library of Congress Cataloging-in-Publication Data

A catalog record for this book is available from the Library of Congress.
Library of Congress Control Number: 2023909748 | ISBN: 979-8-9878343-0-5 (ebook) |
ISBN: 979-8-9878343-1-2 (paperback) | ISBN: 979-8-9878343-2-9 (print)

Unless otherwise noted, Scripture references are taken from the ESV Bible.

Any internet addresses (website, blogs, etc.) and telephone numbers in this book are offered as a resource. They are not intended in any way to be or imply an endorsement from Called Creatives Publishing, not does Called Creatives Publishing vouch for the content of these sites and numbers for the life of this book.

Published in association with Called Creatives Publishing, www.calledcreativespublishing.com

Cover design: *Called Creatives Publishing*
Interior design: *Cody Andras*

2023 – First Edition

Dedication

To Wren—my niece.
And to every other little girl who has given me
the joy of being "Aunt Cody."

May you know that the Jesus by *her* side is the Jesus by *your* side.
May you know that He delights in you.
May you know the peace and joy of His Presence.
May you forever long to know and love Him more.

Table of Contents

Introduction

What does it mean to dwell in the presence of our Creator? To look into the face of our Master? To kneel at His feet? To rest in Him? We talk about being in the presence of God. We hear others talk of it, and we wonder what they mean. We long for it even if we don't know how to define it. Even if we believe that it is possible, it is sometimes hard to imagine what it might look like in our everyday.

I am convinced that God's plan has forever been to usher us into His presence. From before the creation of the world, He was prepared not only to *send* a Savior but to *be* the Savior. He was prepared to dwell among us in order that we might dwell with Him. He dressed Himself in human form and frailty and submitted Himself to a sinner's death. Through the sacrifice of the very Son of God, a way has been opened for us to come boldly before His throne (Hebrews 4:14-16). He delights to know us and to make Himself known. I am convinced that we are welcome. I am not always sure what that means.

I read of the women in the gospels, the ones who encountered Jesus face to face – the ones who sat at His feet, clung to His robe, and sought Him in the crowd. I think that nothing would make me braver than to wrap my arms around the Man of Christ, to sit beside Him, to feel His hands upon my head as He speaks healing and comfort and peace.

But that very Man has promised us something even better. Jesus said to His closest followers, "I tell you the truth: it is to your advantage that I go away, for if I do not go away, the Helper will not come to you. But if I go, I will send Him to you" (John 16:7). Jesus spoke of the Holy Spirit who dwells within everyone who calls upon the saving name of Christ (1 Corinthians 3:16).

The presence of the Living God encloses Himself in our fragile hearts. Yes, the Lord is near. No, He will never leave us nor forsake us.

He is right beside us, but sometimes He is so very hard to find.

What is it to seek the presence of one we cannot see? What does that look like in my life? What does it look like in yours? What does it mean to really live a life that is aware of His presence, that looks for Him, that longs for Him? What does it mean to draw near to God and allow Him to draw near to us (James 4:8)?

I love the stories of Jesus' encounters with the ancient women of the Gospels. Jesus wrapped Himself in flesh and walked beside them. The heart of the Father beat within the skin of the Son and walked beside His daughters.

The Father's heart hasn't changed. The love of the Son hasn't shifted. The Holy Spirit still dwells in our midst. Our God is as wildly committed to your healing and your freedom as He was 2000 years ago, and in these chapters we will watch the Man of Christ move among those ancient women, so that we can recognize the Spirit of Christ as He moves among us.

The Jesus by her side is still the one beside us – the one by your side.

I pray you will take time with these stories in the Gospels. I pray you will spend more time reading the accounts of Jesus in His Word than you do in my words. Each chapter will include the Scripture reference for the encounter we'll consider, and I want to challenge you to read and ponder those stories on your own before you read my reflections. At the end of each chapter, you'll find a simple prayer prompt to where you are invited to engage with the Lord yourself. Don't skip that part! He longs to reveal Himself to you by His Spirit and in His Word. I implore you to take the time to let Him.

May we seek the Spirit of Christ in the same way that these women sought the Man of Christ. May we know what it is to run or fall or laugh or weep in the presence of the one who invites us in. May we encounter Him in ways that we have not. And may our every encounter cause us to love Him more. May we come face to face with an invisible God who once robed Himself in human flesh, and may we find Him to be our Savior and our Lord and our most Faithful Friend.

Respond

Write out Psalm 139:23-24 and 46:10 and put it in a place where you'll see it regularly. As you read through this book, I pray that these verses will serve as a reminder that Jesus is indeed beside you. Each time you see those verses, invite Him to make His presence known to you personally.

Finding Him Faithful

Mundane Moments

Anna

Luke 2:22-40

The thing about new years and new starts is that they end so quickly. There is always a flurry of excitement around 11:58 pm on New Year's Eve: Champagne. Sparklers. Kisses. Cake (if your friends bake – thankfully, mine do!).

And then it's done.

This year, eight o'clock on Tuesday morning looks very similar to eight o'clock on Tuesday morning *last* year. Sure, there are minor adjustments to some of the details. There is a little more energy or renewed determination. But for the most part, a new year is not a magical reset for very long.

Maybe it's not January 1 for you. Maybe it's the start of a new school year. Maybe it's a new journal. Maybe it's the cracking open of a new book. Maybe that's what has led you here.

Perhaps you're opening up these pages because you're desperate for a new encounter with the living God. Fresh starts hold potential and perspective, but new (by its very nature) never lasts long.

The new quickly fades. By January 15, the new journal has a frayed corner. The tip of the new lipstick smashed into the lid.

The new plan has suffered a slight setback. Your new book's cover has a water ring from a cup of iced coffee. Nothing is broken yet, but there are signs of wear.

It's a bit of a relief. It releases some of the pressure.

We can stop worrying about ruining it. Instead, we can remember to live it – to enjoy the million little moments that make up a day. To live even these moments that we'll soon forget. To let them be mundane and to let that be okay.

It makes me think about a woman named Anna.

Anna was an eighty-four-year-old widow whose life revolved around the House of the Lord. Luke called her "a prophetess" (Luke 2:36). Whether she lived within the Temple grounds or centered her life around that holy place, the Word of God tells us that "She did not depart from the temple, worshiping with fasting and prayer night and day" (Luke 2:37). And she lived that way for most of her life.

But one day, her life intersected with the Man of Christ, or more accurately, with the infant Christ.

She was going about her day, cultivating faithfulness as she had for many years. She was doing the things she knew to do. She was doing what was before her, even when others didn't, even when it wasn't fancy, even when it wasn't seen. Perhaps even when it was a little bit boring.

"And coming up at that very hour" (Luke 2:38).

At what very hour? At the very hour that a young couple carried their newborn into the temple – Mary and Joseph brought the Son of God into the House of God.

Take a moment and let that settle in. It's a big deal.

The King had come. The glory of God was wrapped in flesh, and his parents laid Him in the arms of a man named Simeon, who proclaimed Him to be the Savior: "My eyes have seen your salvation that you have prepared in the presence of all peoples, a light for revelation to the Gentiles, and for glory to your people Israel" (Luke 2:30-32).

At that very hour, Anna walked up. It was the holiest of hours. How many hours had she walked the same path? How many hours had she knelt in the same place? How many hours had she trusted what she could not see? How many hours were made up of moments that blended into the next? How many hours did she spend cultivating a life of faithfulness that few would ever see?

And then *that* hour.

Anna recognized the face of God in the infant's wrinkled forehead. Perhaps she looked into the squinting eyes of the one for whom she'd waited, of the one whom she had worshiped and served. Maybe she kissed the top of His head and whispered love and thanks and praise.

That hour. And then it passed. It's likely that the next day looked a lot like the one before. But Anna had seen Jesus. Her days might have been the same afterward, but she would never be.

Long years of faithful moments had tendered Anna's heart to recognize the faithful face of God.

Might this year and its moments leave us tender toward Him too?

As we go from the laundry room to the kitchen for the fourteenth time. As we make the thousandth copy. As we smear peanut butter on the child's sandwich. As we read. As we send the email or the text or the letter. As we let the dog out. As we drive to the place we are needed or to the place we want to be. As we do whatever it is we do on the most mundane of days.

Might we recognize Him when we see Him?
Might we trust Him even when we don't?
Might we seek and find Him faithful?

Respond

1. How do you typically respond to new starts? Even beginning a book can be a fresh start. What are you hoping to find in starting this book?
2. Psalm 37:3 says, "Trust in the Lord and do good; dwell in the land and cultivate faithfulness" (NASB, 1995). What would it look like in your own life to cultivate faithfulness in your mundane moments so that you'll recognize Christ in those moments when He appears so clearly? Where and how can you position yourself to be present and attentive when He shows up?

Ask the Lord to make you more aware of His presence as you seek Him through this study. Ask Him to help you recognize and to respond to Him more quickly. Carry a piece of paper or a journal throughout this week, and write down moments when you see the Lord, however small or mundane they may seem.

Bothering the Savior

Peter's Mother-in-Law

Luke 4:38-40

I have a habit of ranking problems. My system resembles the triage setup at the site of an emergency. I'll slap green, yellow, or red bands on problems, declaring which are fit for help and which I can handle just fine. Red is for sure going to Jesus. We'll deal with yellow after all the red has been handled. And green? Well, I'll handle green with the energy I have left.

In a crisis, this system is efficient. But as a lifestyle, it's not good.

The family emergency? The middle of the night phone call? The questionable results of the medical scan? Those are definitely going to Jesus. And if everything else is going well, then the dilemma at work, the frustration toward a friend, or the quiet fear of the future might get taken to Jesus as well.

But not the hand I burned on the stovetop. Not the overwhelm I feel when the number of copies I need to make is more than the amount of time I have before school. Not the calendaring conundrum of scheduling home repairs. I won't "bother" Jesus with those. Instead, I hold them close and squash them down, handling them in my own way and my own strength.

I deny myself the help of Christ because those problems seem too small or insignificant. I run myself ragged, trying to prove myself capable. Eventually, I break under the tiny trials because the one who came to save the world also cares deeply about the details of my daily life.

If this book weren't exclusively about the women Jesus encountered in His time upon the earth, Jesus' disciple Peter would feature prominently. I love Peter. I love that he said what he thought. I love that he moved on quickly when Jesus corrected him. I love that he could fly from one extreme to the next without warning. I love that he knew who Jesus was, and I love that he also failed, again and again, to be the man he intended to be.

In his own strength, Peter came up short every time.

Since Peter isn't a woman, we're going to focus on three verses found in Luke 4:38-40 about Peter's mother-in-law. It's important to note that Jesus didn't call Peter to be His disciple until after the exchange we're going to look at here (Luke 5:1-11).

Very early in His ministry, Jesus entered Capernaum and began teaching (Luke 4:31). Capernaum was a small, lakeside town along the Sea of Galilee. While Jesus was teaching, a demon-possessed man came, and the demonic spirit cried out, taunting Jesus (Luke 4:34). Jesus rebuked the spirit and drove the demon out of the man, restoring his health and sanity.

Luke reports, unsurprisingly, that the people were filled with wonder and amazement, marveling that Jesus could command even the spirit world with such power and authority (Luke 4:36-37).

When Jesus left the synagogue, He entered Peter's home where Peter's mother-in-law lay in bed with a fever. When He entered, "They appealed to him on her behalf" (Luke 4:38).

In my triage system, I would have been trying to decide whether her fever was high enough to warrant an appeal to Jesus. I would have been weighing her illness against the severity of the need of the demon-possessed man. I would have been trying to decide whether her body was headed toward recovery, and I only would have bothered Jesus if she seemed to get worse.

And there is the problem: That pesky word – *bothered*.

I am still tempted to try not to *bother* the Christ.

Was the Man of Christ bothered by this woman's need? No. To my surprise, the Spirit-breathed Word of God doesn't record how sick she was, how long it had been, or if any family members had tried simple remedies to deal with the fever themselves. The Word of God only records that Jesus went, stood over her, and rebuked the fever. (Luke 4:39)

Peter's mother-in-law rose – healed – and began to serve. (Luke 4:39)

The Man of Christ treated the sick woman the same way He treated the demon-possessed man. He rebuked what was harassing her, and He set her free. And after that, Scripture says that all those who were sick "with various diseases" were brought to Him, and Jesus healed them.

Why do I think the Spirit of Christ would respond any differently to me?

Why do I think He expects me to measure my requests and prove their significance before I lay them at His feet? Why do I think Jesus expects me not to bother Him?

A Day is coming when the Man of Christ, who humbly walked among humanity, will return in all His glory. When He does, He will end sickness, death, and disease. Every single thing that is out of line with His perfect design for creation will be rebuked, and Jesus will restore us all with the same compassion He had for Peter's mother-in-law.

Jesus will set right everything that has gone wrong.

Until that Day, we still get to come to Jesus. We get to cry out to Him. He hasn't left us here to "make the best of it" or to "look on the bright side" or to "triage our needs."

Instead, He invites us to lay before Him with our fevers regardless of their severity. We are invited to find Him faithful to meet both our desperate and our daily needs.

One Day, Christ will fully rebuke all that harasses God's children.

On this side of that final restoration, some fevers will still spike, but when they do, the Spirit of Christ will stand beside our bedside 'til we're well.

Respond

1. Can you relate to my tendency to rank or triage problems? What type of problems in your life do you believe don't warrant the care and help of the Lord? How do you typically try to hand those?

2. Is there a specific problem (or problems) you have been trying not to "bother" the Lord with? Why?

Take a moment now to invite the Spirit into any problems you may have dismissed as too small or insignificant to ask Him into. Confess that you have been trying to handle them on your own, and intentionally involve the Holy Spirit in those specific places in your life. Ask for His perspective, intervention, wisdom, and presence.

Unburdened

The Bent-Over Woman

Luke 13:10-17

We often try to stand beneath burdens we were not meant to bear.

Sometimes a tragedy pushes us to that place. Sometimes it is one too many lesser pains. Sometimes it is the sting of another's words spoken in haste, and sometimes it is ominous silence in an area of desperate need. Doubt invades, and discouragement hangs heavy. Faith may linger for a moment, but it soon feels artificial – a distant memory from a different time.

We square our shoulders to the world and brace ourselves for an inevitable hit. Or we turn our heads for a moment, blindsided by what we could not have seen coming. We lock our knees to keep them from giving way beneath us, and it isn't long before the lightheadedness sets in.

We finally bend to keep from breaking and realize we cannot stand back up. We thought our backbones were stronger. We thought our faith was firmer.

I can't say for sure, but I suspect that the woman in our story today knew something of this struggle.

The bent-over woman (I do wish we had been told her name) doesn't appear to have approached Christ with any great boldness or expectation. We're told Jesus was teaching in a synagogue, and she was just there. Eighteen years is a long time to be harassed by the same illness and bound by the same spirit. I wonder if she had abandoned all hope of healing. Had hearing that Christ was in her town awakened in her a desire that had lain dormant beneath the reality of daily life? I wonder if she crept into the back of the synagogue that day with some vestige of hope that He would see her. Even as that hope stirred, did she fear the disappointment if the Lord failed to act?

Perhaps the most refreshing element of this woman's story is the one-sidedness of Christ's compassion – His faithfulness without any indication of her great faith. If you come into the Lord's presence today with unshakable and fervent faith, I'm so glad. But we don't always come with confident expectation and sturdy hope. Sometimes we are simply grateful to find ourselves in a room where Christ's Spirit happens to be, and it takes all the faith we have to hope that He might notice we are here.

No matter your current level of faith, take heart as you reread Luke's words:

> When Jesus saw her, He called her over and said to her, "Woman, you are freed from your disability." And He laid His hands on her, and immediately she was made straight, and she glorified God. (Luke 13:12-13)

Jesus *saw* her. Might she have drawn her first deep breath in that moment? I might have.

Jesus sees you, and He sees what weighs on you. He sees the circumstance that has outlasted your resolve. It may be a seemingly small area. It may be the biggest need you've ever faced. It may be a subtle, mocking fear that your life somehow does not warrant God's tending.

As He did for that woman who walked the earth two thousand years ago, He calls you to Himself. She must have shuffled, still bent over, toward the Man who beckoned her. So even if you stumble under the weight that's landed heavy, you can choose to make your way to Him.

Faith is sometimes displayed in our choice to come when Jesus calls. We have a choice. We can choose *not* to make our way to Him. We can choose not to move for fear of what others will think if they see us shuffling to Jesus' side. We might choose the familiar burden over the unknown risk of the Savior's intervention. We might choose anger toward the God we blame, toward the only one who sees us. We may accuse Him of not intervening sooner and of not *preventing* this burden in the first place. We might choose the convenience of the handicap we've grown accustomed to. Sometimes our burdens are working for us. Sometimes our burdens have replaced our backbones, and we can't imagine life without them. What if we no longer had this excuse? What if we no longer harbored this hate? Sometimes our affliction has blurred with our identity to the degree that we don't know who we'd be without it.

The bent-over woman in our story took the risk. She had the courage to make her way to the Man who had called her to Himself.

When she got to Him, Jesus laid His hands on her, and "she was made straight" (Luke 13:13). I love that God Almighty, wrapped in flesh, called her close enough to Himself that He could lay His hands on her. I love that as she straightened to stand for the first time in eighteen years, she looked into the face of God. The woman in our story didn't encounter someone who was "sweet" or "kind." He offered more than empty platitudes. She encountered one who was powerful enough to extend healing and strength to her weakness – to free her from what had ensnared her.

The risk was worth it. She encountered the one who could restore her and who had come near enough to do it.

By His Spirit, Christ can do the same for us. He is able, and He is willing. Come find life in your Father's presence. I have felt the weight of discouragement and doubt too deeply to dismiss it lightly, but I have also encountered the Lord's tender compassion too personally not to speak of it. He sees what threatens to overwhelm. And He cares so much. He is powerful and good and merciful enough to do something about it. Don't just take my word for it. Come into His presence and see His goodness for yourself.

Dare to approach the one who can steady you to stand.

Let Him tend to you. Whether He changes your circumstances or meets with you in the midst of them, the Lord is the only one who can heal you, the only one who can free you from what sits heavy on your shoulders.

The Spirit of Christ doesn't just tell you to stand. He invites you to *come*. He places His hands upon your shoulders and lifts you. He tilts your face to look to His.

I pray the Lord encourages you this week. I pray you find Him faithful. I pray He speaks to your heart in a way only He can. I pray you have the courage to hobble toward His call. I pray you rest in His freedom and healing. I pray that today, regardless of your circumstance, you will taste His presence and know He is good!

Respond

1. Are there any hopes or desires that you've silenced to avoid disappointment? What burden does Jesus see weighing most heavily on you?
2. What might hold you back from approaching Him with what has weighed you down? What do you fear might happen if you release the burden you've become accustomed to carrying?

He has called you from the crowd. What would it look like to respond to His call – to come forward and meet Him face to face? Think practically. Do you need to set aside time to meet with Him? Do you need to confess a sin or shame that has held you back from Him for too long? Do you need to tell Him what has wounded you? Could you meet Him in worship the way you used to – or the way you long to? What would it look like for you to respond to Him the way this woman did? What would it look like to make your way to Him?

Inviting Him In

Martha

Luke 10:38-42

Irritation surged as her shin grazed her sister's unmoving frame. She sighed as she let the spoon land against the bowl, making a little more noise than necessary. Didn't her sister know how badly she wanted to hear the words Jesus spoke? Didn't her sister realize she'd left her alone to bear the burden of host? Martha was understandably annoyed: "Lord, do you not care that my sister has left me to serve alone? Tell her then to help me" (Luke 10:40).

"Martha, Martha, you are anxious and troubled about many things, but one thing is necessary. Mary has chosen the good portion, which will not be taken away from her" (Luke 10:41-42).

Don't let anyone tell you that Mary loved Jesus more. Might Martha's annoyance partly have been that she wished she were seated beside her sister? Might she have longed to set down the dishtowel and enjoy the presence of the one she'd invited in? Did you catch that? It was *Martha* who asked Jesus to come into her home: "a woman named Martha welcomed [Jesus] into her house" (Luke 10:38).

Yes, Mary chose the better thing.

But Martha was the reason that the "better thing" was in their home!

What would make Martha nearly miss the one she had invited in?

I can't say for sure, but I can tell you why *I've* missed Him. I can tell you why I've run frantically from oven to sink rather than rest at the feet of my God. I can tell you why I've fought furiously to keep moving when the Spirit inside me is whispering, "S*low down."*

I am afraid He might have come only for the meal I promised Him.

I am afraid He might not enjoy my presence as much as I enjoy His.

I am afraid He might like my sister more.

I am afraid that if I sit down to listen, He might stand to leave.

Maybe Martha busied her hands to distract her spirit from nagging fears. Maybe she kept her distance in a strange attempt to keep Him near.

And all the while, He just wanted *her*.

I sat at an unrushed lunch a few weeks ago and told a trusted friend things I didn't realize I had been thinking or feeling. I found that I kept talking because she kept listening. It is a tender thing to realize that someone has the time to *be* with you.

But it is a vulnerable thing too. The small talk inevitably runs out. And in the silence, you find that the deeper things begin to surface. When you have nothing "of value" left to offer, you realize that *you* are the thing of value.

Mary knew this to be true. So she sat still in the presence of her Lord. And even as I write this, I can hear our world's response: Maybe she didn't have all the responsibilities that her sister shouldered. Maybe she was less involved. Maybe she didn't realize all that she was leaving undone. Maybe she just had more time than Martha.

Yeah, maybe. Or maybe she *took* the time. Perhaps she realized that her worth was not bound in her service. Maybe she knew how much Jesus enjoyed her presence.

Maybe that brought the kind of freedom we can hardly fathom.

In a world where lack of time is a status symbol, I have found myself frantically *filling* my time instead of intentionally *taking* my time to delight, to rest, to sit still at the feet of the one I long to enjoy. To let Him speak. To learn His voice.

I have fought against those things because stillness feels unimportant. And that makes *me* feel unimportant. Yes, that's it. It makes me feel insignificant to say that my day had moments not filled with productivity.

Martha forgets that she is *loved*, so she fights to prove that she is *important*.

We are crying out – in as many different ways as there are humans – for someone to tell us that we're worthy. And a voice cries out from the cross in the middle of an ancient crowd, "It is finished!" (John 19:30).

May we silence the frantic rush of lives that scream back to the bloodied Savior, "No, it's not!"

Because it is. The declaration has been made. We may feel unworthy or insignificant. Others may tell us, in word or glance, that we don't amount to much, but the nail-scarred hands and the spear-pierced side of the Son of God say otherwise. Jesus Christ hung on the cross, and He gave up His Spirit so that the

Father might pour out that Spirit into the hearts of His children: "And because you are sons, God has sent the Spirit of His Son into our hearts, crying, 'Abba! Father!'" (Galatians 4:6).

We can lean back, be loved, and find our worth in the steady rhythm of our Father's faithful heart.

Every Martha can drop to her knees beside her sister and enjoy the company of the one that she invited in.

We find He didn't only come for the meal we promised Him.

We find He enjoys our presence just as much as we enjoy His.

We find He loves us as much as He loves our sister.

We find it was never our distance that was keeping Him near.

We find Him faithful though we feared He might not be.

Respond

1. What makes you afraid to settle in the presence of the Lord? If you are honest, why do you fear that He might not meet you when you seek Him?
2. What do you tend to turn to and how do you fill your time when you feel unimportant? How can we let those tendencies become warning signs that alert us to the fact that we are feeling unimportant or insecure? When we are tempted to turn to those old habits and ways, could we turn instead to the Lord?

CODY ANDRAS

Set aside some time this week to rest in the presence of the Lord. Don't bring your phone or your journal or even your Bible. Find a quiet place and sit down alone. Don't worry about making conversation with God. Acknowledge that you've come to rest in Him. Ask Him to teach you what that means. Ask Him to teach you how to rest. And then do it. Rest. Relax. Close your eyes. Enjoy your God. Trust that He enjoys you too.

Faithfulness in the Flesh

Mary and Elizabeth

Luke 1:26-56

As we sat there, she said, "I get it." And I knew that was true. I knew that I could say the same to her. Our circumstances were similar enough without being identical. Our seasons were the same kind of strange. Her eyes mirrored my puzzled hope, squinting through a layer of weariness. I knew I could share my doubts because she would not mistake them for faithlessness. I knew that her joy wasn't a mask but also that her hurt was real. I knew that the two could coexist in a crazy, awkward kind of way.

So, when she said, "I get it," I didn't slap her. Because it was the truth, and it was such a gift.

I didn't offer her any bizarre platitudes, and she didn't offer me any unsolicited advice. We just sat there. We laughed at the absurdities. We shared the words we had and sat in the silence that words couldn't fill.

Perhaps you've known the tenderness of a similar moment.

Perhaps you've seen the faithfulness of God in the flesh of a friend.

When the angel Gabriel appeared to Mary, she was "thoroughly shaken" (Luke 1:29, MSG). Who wouldn't be? I smile when I think of God. Just six months prior, He'd sent Gabriel to a very old man whose dream of children had died a quiet death, a man who didn't dare hope that what the angel said could be true. This time, I imagine God pulling Gabriel aside again, pointing to a girl who slipped her feet into well-worn sandals and went about her day in an unimpressive town. I smile because I bet He smiled. *That one*, God might have whispered to the angel – voice thick with emotion – *will bear My Son*. And Gabriel's heart might have quickened, if angels have hearts that do such things, as Mary kept walking through her tired town.

Until the angel appeared to her. Until he told her she would bear a son. Until he told her she would bear *the* Son.

Then she had questions. (Most virgins would.) But she didn't doubt. Somehow she didn't even waver. I don't know if angels have hearts that beat loudly and fast, but I know women do. And I bet Mary's did. I bet adrenaline surged through the body that would bear the Christ. I bet she looked into that majestic angel's eyes and thought things she wouldn't have dared speak to him. I bet her faith soared, but I bet her knees shook.

Thoroughly shaken. Yes, I imagine that she was.

"And did you know that your cousin Elizabeth conceived a son, old as she is?" Gabriel asked her (Luke 1:36).

And did you know that you are not alone?

God, in all His glorious might and majestic splendor, sent an angel to proclaim the miraculous conception of the Messiah. The Son of God would confine Himself to skin and sinew. The Lord of all creation would bend down to become a part of it. His eyelids and arteries and fingerprints would be knit together in the womb of this woman. His blood would mingle with hers.

Mary would be the mother of God. But she would also always be His daughter.

And so, right before Gabriel left God to go to Mary, I think maybe God touched the angel's shoulder and said, "*Make sure she knows about Elizabeth. Make sure My daughter knows she's not alone.*"

"And did you know that your cousin Elizabeth conceived a son, old as she is?" (Luke 1:36, MSG)

Who would take this tender time with His child? Only the most tender Father. Only the most compassionate God.

"Mary didn't waste a minute" after the angel left her. "She got up and traveled to a town in Judah in the hill country, straight to Zechariah's house, and greeted Elizabeth." (Luke 1:39-20, MSG) Because women need each other.

Elizabeth recognized the heavy hand of God upon her cousin. Mary shared her heart with Elizabeth in a way she might have hesitated to share with anyone else. The virgin and the barren one watched their bellies swell with sons, and they marveled at the power of God. Laughter. Stories. Silence. A few of those wide-eyed glances that express a question without demanding an answer.

For three months, they spent their days together and reminded each other that God was who He claimed to be. When Mary, who could not yet feel the Son of God kick within her, began to wonder if it was real, she placed her hand on Elizabeth to feel John's foot press against her palm. When Elizabeth's energy faltered and anxiety threatened, she looked at the fresh face of Mary to find her footing.

Faith shared. Hope borrowed. Belief renewed.

Perhaps you need to hear your Father's gentle reminder: *You're not alone.* "Do you know about Elizabeth?" Maybe you need to run to her home. Maybe you need, as Elizabeth did, to open your home to the Mary on your doorstep.

May you recognize the hand of God upon your sister. May you see His call and His grace and His love for her, and may it remind you that He feels the same toward you. May her hope renew yours.

May her presence remind you of His.

And may her faith reassure you of His faithfulness.

Respond

1. What do you believe is the difference between having questions and having doubts? Can you think of an example of each in your current circumstances? Take some time to lay those doubts and questions out before the Lord, asking Him for help to understand what He'll reveal and for help to trust Him even with what you cannot understand.

2. When has your faith been encouraged, built up, or sustained by the faith of another?

Ask the Lord if there is a friend or acquaintance in your life that you need to reach out to – either to seek encouragement or to offer it in the kind hand of friendship. When He brings someone to mind, respond. Our Father gives good gifts to His daughters, and sometimes, His best gift is the gift of each other.

The Exchange of Shame

The Woman at the Well

John 4:1-42

She came burdened and alone. More than alone, actually: She was isolated, having been shunned often enough that she had willfully withdrawn. But in the heat of that day, when no one was likely to be at the well, she came face to face with the one she certainly would not have expected to greet her – Jesus.

Samaria and Judea were both originally part of Israel, the land God promised to Abraham and his descendants (Genesis 15:18-31). The Israelites conquered and settled that land under the leadership of Joshua. After a time as a unified kingdom, Israel was divided into the Northern and Southern Kingdoms. The Northern Kingdom retained the name Israel, and the Southern Kingdom was called Judah. In 722 BC, the Northern Kingdom of Israel fell to the Assyrians. Years later, Babylon took the Southern Kingdom of Judah into captivity in 596 BC.

When the Assyrians conquered the Northern Kingdom, the land was filled with foreigners. Some Northern Israelites were carried into captivity, but many remained and intermarried with the foreigners. Their lives and religion blended with the pagan people, and they became known as the Samaritans. When the Jews of the Southern Kingdom returned from their captivity to rebuild Jerusalem and the Temple, they refused to associate with their Samaritan neighbors to the north because they viewed them as compromised people.

Centuries later, during the time of Christ, the schism still existed between the Jews and the Samaritans. Jews refused to associate with Samaritans, as it would have made the Jews "unclean" even to share a vessel of water with them. It was common for Jews traveling from Galilee (north of Samaria) to Judea (south of Samaria) to go far out of the way to avoid traveling through Samaria.

Yet, Jesus marched right through Samaria. And His Spirit still does the same today. He still strolls boldly through the landscape we think He is most likely to avoid – our shortcomings and shame, our inconsistencies and inadequacies. He doesn't walk the long way around as the others do. He walks right through the middle.

The Messiah didn't hurry through the rough terrain of Samaria. Instead, He rested beside an ancient well and dared to ask for a drink.

Even if the woman at the well had been the most upstanding citizen, it would have been unorthodox for Jesus to speak with her. But she was not upstanding. To the Jews, she bore the stigma of Samaritan, and even within Samaria, she bore the stigma of disgrace. Still, Jesus chose to sit face to face with the most unlikely of people at the most unlikely of times in the most unlikely of places.

"Go, call your husband, and come here" (John 4:17), Jesus said to her. Her face flushed with failure. I can almost feel my cheeks warm as well.

It's one thing to talk about the sins of our pasts – those decisions we've made that we wouldn't make again. But what we do with our present failings is another story. What *I* do with my present failings is another story. I hide them and disguise them. I make excuses for them and hope the Lord will remain oblivious until I can clean myself up.

Jesus, however, didn't wait for the Samaritan woman to get her life in order. He met her right in the middle of her present shame. He brought it up right there in broad daylight.

His Spirit still points with the same uncompromising kindness to the sin and shame I try so hard to hide. He doesn't point out my sin to drive me farther into shame or isolation. He brings it up as one who longs to lift it.

When Jesus first spoke of living water, the Samaritan woman asked for it, hoping she would not have to return to the well. Isolation still appealed to her. Shame still covered her head, but the Giver of Life sought to hide her shame. After their conversation, the woman was changed. She forgot herself. She forgot her shame and her isolation. She dropped her burden in exchange for His. Carrying the gospel to a desperate world, she ran to the people she had avoided and invited them, "Come!" (John 4:28-29)

He "told [her] everything [she had] ever done" (John 4:28), and she found it reason for rejoicing.

The woman at the well found life in exchange for her sin and shame. She found the Messiah.

The faithful Lifter of your head leans toward you with the same tender conviction. Can you sense the Messiah nearby? He reaches His hand toward you, and you drop your chin to your chest, hoping He will not notice that embarrassment climbs red up your neck. But then you feel His gentle hand. He cups your face in His fingers. He lifts your chin to look at Him.

Instead of the furious wrath you expected, you find forgiveness and acceptance. You find that you can't outrun the faithful love of this Father.

The Spirit of the one who sat beside the well now sits beside us in our shame. With tender mercy, He asks if we might like to taste the living water.

He's wondering if we might like to be free. He asks if we might like to be healed.

James 5:16 tells us to "confess [our] sins to one another and pray for one another, that [we] may be healed."

We squirm. *Isn't there some other way? Perhaps one that doesn't require the awkward uncovering of our fears and failures in the noonday sun?*

Christ has forgiven us completely, yet shame still smothers us. The taunts of "if anyone knew..." tempt us to hide behind the false security of "...but they don't know." So we wrap our wounds tighter and tuck them away. We hope we'll get better even if we'll never be well. But that tourniquet-tight wrap cuts off the circulation, and something dies that once was ours. Our hope. Our passion. Our relationship. Our laughter.

We resign ourselves to death and learn to live without whatever we have lost until the hope of healing finally outweighs the fear.

Several years ago, I sat on my couch on Good Friday and mumbled a confession I didn't want to make. One of my closest friends sat across from me, unable to lift the shame of sin but confident in the God who could. And as I admitted my failure, she did something I didn't expect — she unwrapped her wounds and laid her own mistakes where I could see them. Then she prayed, and as she did, something inside me beat back to life. As confident as I had been of my complete forgiveness in the presence of God alone, I hadn't known how desperately I needed the healing that came in the presence and prayers of another.

The Bible calls the Church the body of Christ for a reason. My friend's hugs and prayers and presence were the hugs and prayers and presence of Christ.

The Spirit of Christ sometimes sits beside us at the well, wearing the faithful flesh of one of His children. He lifts our shame. He sets us free. We find that He knows everything we've ever done, and we find that He loves us anyway.

And we leave the well rejoicing!

Respond

1. We all have a Samaria of our own. What shortcomings and inadequacies do you fear might disqualify you from a life with the Lord? What parts of yourself (your personality, background, etc.) are you tempted to hide from God and His people? Have you ever encountered the Spirit of God in that place of your life? How has it changed you? Ask Him to make Himself known in that area. He is not afraid to meet you in the middle of Samaria.

2. Is there any present sin in your life that you have not yet confessed in the presence of Christ? You are seen and known,

and that is reason for rejoicing. He has done all that was necessary to welcome you into His presence. You need only come and confess. Find the one who will tell you everything you have ever done, and then be faithful to forgive you. Find the one whose shed blood covers all your shame.

Is there anything that you are hiding? Any secrets you are keeping for fear of "if anyone knew"? If shame has isolated you from fellowship with God or other believers, take a deep breath, reach out to a trusted friend or mentor who can handle your sin, and ask him or her to pray with you as you confess. I can almost guarantee that it will be painful and awkward and uncomfortable. I can also promise that it will bring healing. It really will be worth it.

Presenting Our Problems

Mary at the Wedding of Cana

John 2:1-12

A name like *Cody* distinguishes me in a room full of women. In fact, except for the rodeo where a shocking percentage of bull riders share my name, I'm almost always the only *Cody* in the room. Growing up, I saw this as a severe hardship, especially when other kids would look at me funny: "Cody? That's a boy's name."

Well, I'm not a boy. And that's my name.

I told someone recently that one of the trickiest parts of writing a book about the women Jesus encountered in the gospels is that many are unnamed, and half are named Mary.

The beautiful thing about our Savior is that these women were never "just another Mary" to Him. There was Mary and Mary and Mary, and while their names on His lips might have sounded the same to the passersby, I like to think that perhaps they could tell which one He meant simply by His intonation.

I don't know if that's true, but I'm confident that this Mary – the one we're about to witness with Jesus at a wedding in Cana – recognized the way He said her name.

To Jesus, this Mary wasn't "Mary." She was "Mom."

In John 2, Jesus is at a wedding with His mom when she informed Him that the family had run out of wine. She didn't directly ask Him to solve the problem, but her presentation of the problem implied that she expected Jesus to intervene.

I want to start by clearing something up. Jesus is quoted in John 2:4 as addressing his mother as "Woman." To our western ears, this likely sounds highly disrespectful. We are used to seeing it in a context such as this:

"Woman, leave me alone."

"Woman, get back in your place."

"Woman, back off."

It's disconcerting (to say the least) to imagine Jesus speaking this way to any woman, let alone His mother! The word itself is indeed best translated as "woman," but it's important to note that the term was "highly respectful and affectionate."[1]

No one seems quite sure what to make of this exchange when you read the commentators' thoughts on this passage. Everyone agrees that Jesus meant no disrespect, but they differ in interpretation about what Mary was asking of Jesus, why she was asking it, and whether she was out of line for asking.

Since "the experts" can't decide, I've excused myself from the role of judge. Regardless of the nuances of this mother-son exchange, Mary knew her Son was able. She knew He could be trusted. She knew He would do good.

---

[1] Marvin Richardson Vincent, *Word Studies in the New Testament*. (New York: Charles Scribner's Sons, 1887), 2:80.

And Jesus did. He did exactly what His mother asked: He solved the problem.

Jesus changed the water meant for purification into wine ordained for celebration. He provided what the people lacked. He salvaged the honor and dignity of the host, which would have been at stake had the guests realized the wedding host's embarrassing lack.

When the servants took the new wine to the head waiter, he was astounded by the quality of the wine. In his amazement, the waiter declared to the groom: "Everyone serves the good wine first, and when people have drunk freely, then the poor wine. But you have kept the good wine until now" (John 2:10).

Neither the servants nor Mary nor Jesus Himself ever announced where the wine had come from. The groom may never have known that the wine had nearly run out. He didn't know that Jesus had quietly preserved his family's dignity.

The only ones recorded as witnesses of this first miracle of Jesus were His mother and His disciples.

It was a tensely tender moment between mother and Son.

In the end, Jesus proved to be exactly the one His mother believed Him to be.

Mary may not have known the means Jesus would use, but she knew the grace He would extend.

She may not have known *how* Jesus would work, but she knew *who* Jesus was. And so she felt free to approach Him, even perhaps when she "shouldn't" have. She sought His help even when it might not have been "appropriate." She took Him her problems, even when the world (and the commentaries-to-come) might question her "rightness."

If Mary is at fault here, her fault is too much faith in her Son.

At the end of the day – and throughout the day – I'd like to be known for taking too much to my Savior. I want to feel free to lay my troubles at His feet even if I'm unsure what He'll do with them. I want to turn around and cry out "Jesus," even when the world thinks I should instead use logic or common sense or my God-given resources to solve a problem.

I want to be faulted for too much faith in the Son.

Last week, I made a list of reasons I am tired, of reasons I'd like to curl up on the couch and zone out to the noise of the television set. Some weighty items are on the list: a child's medical crisis, a dear friend's loss, a relational conflict between people I love. I can't do a thing about any of it. At the bottom of that list, but at the top of my to-dos, one item threatened to push me right over the edge of sanity: "the broken gutter."

At the beginning of the week, my neighbor's tree snapped in half and blew into the side of my house in the middle of the night. Thankfully it was a palm tree, and the damage was limited to the gutter. But it's been a real hassle dealing with neighbors, workmen, and ladder access.

I don't know how to handle it – any of it, but it's the broken gutter that's staring me down and wearing me out. Normally efficient and decisive, I've been paralyzed, and it's been setback after setback as I've tried to get it fixed.

I haven't taken it to Jesus because I don't know what He could do about it.

But neither did His mom.

All she knew was that, in the moment's need, Jesus was the one *she* needed to intervene.

She knew He *would* do what He could. And she knew He *could* do what was necessary.

We don't have to take Jesus our proposed solutions. He invites us to come before Him with our unsolved problems, spiritual and practical needs, and our confident (if confused) faith that He has the solution we cannot see.

I get to hand Him that last line item on my list: "My gutter is broken."

I want to have ideas or suggestions or a specific request. But, for a myriad of reasons, I don't. I want to know the ending of the story. I wish I could tell you how Jesus has come through, but I'm still standing here like Mary, praying for the faith she had when she looked at those servants standing nearby and said, "Do whatever He tells you to do." She knew He would come through, so she confidently displayed her faith even before she had His answer.

So, as His mother did, I present the problem and stand back to see what He will do.

Some people (maybe you're one of them) will think this sounds lazy, trite, or immature. But those people don't get to decide whether I should take this trouble to the God I trust.

His mother took her trouble to her Son, and as His daughters, we get to take our troubles to our Father. We get to trust that He knows what to do about the problems that have made us shrug our shoulders in bewilderment.

We get to watch, in quiet wonder, as Jesus comes through for us in ways the world wasn't sure He would, in ways the world around us may never know He did, and in ways the commentators may not applaud.

We get to find Him faithful to fix what we don't know how to solve.

Respond

1. What do you think about Jesus' response to His mother when she approaches Him with the problem of the wine?
2. Can you recall a time in your life when Jesus met your need, even if you weren't sure how He would do it?

What problems are you currently facing? Perhaps, like me, you need to list what makes you tired. Maybe it's a list of things, or maybe it's just one thing you've been carrying on your own because you aren't sure how to ask Jesus to fix it. What would it look like to present the problem to Him? Can you tell Him about the struggle(s) you face, even if you don't know what He can do about it? Can you, like Mary, trust Him to handle it well, even if you don't yet see the solution?

Receiving Back Our Dead

The Widow of Nain

Luke 7:11-17

"I'm going to give you this ice pack...."

Excuse me? You're going to give me an ice pack?

I was 28 years old. I had gone to urgent care to ensure that my swollen eye didn't mean I had strep or pink eye. I did not need an ice pack!

Frustrated and offended, I bitterly took the ice pack, dumped it in my purse, and headed home from the doctor's office. Looking back, it's possible my reaction was a little intense. It's been known to happen, but I need you to know this about my history with ice packs: Our school nurse used to hand them out when you said you didn't feel well, but you didn't have a fever. The school believed it was compassionate. I found it humiliating.

They thought it said: *We believe you. We're sorry you're not feeling well. We want to help.*

I heard: *We believe that you think you don't feel well. But you're mistaken. You are fine. We are paying you (in freezing-cold currency) to return to class.*

I went to the same school for twelve years. I went to the nurse's office exactly four times. The first time was in the first grade. I had a stomachache, and I wanted to go home. The school nurse gave me an ice pack; I vowed never to return. I was forced to return three times, but these were more "legitimate" reasons: A chalkboard fell on my hand, and the teacher made me go. I got kicked in the eye; the teacher made me go. Finally, as a senior in high school, I was sick enough to go home, and (do you see the pattern?) a teacher made me go.

I know that some kids fake illnesses to try to get sent home. There is a reason for the ice-pack distribution. That is not the point. The point is that somewhere in my childhood, I became afraid of the ice pack response – to the degree that I would not fake illness, but I would fake wellness.

I don't think I was very sick that day as a twenty-eight-year-old in the doctor's office. I was exhausted. I probably needed to go home and sleep. But when the nurse handed me the ice pack, that first-grade stubbornness flared, and instead of taking the rest of the day off, I took a nap and then rallied for the activities I'd planned. I had an invitation from the God of this universe to sit with Him and be still. And I turned it down because of an ice pack and all it meant to me.

That ice pack said that I was fine, that I was overreacting. In my mind, I was being sent back to class. Its dripping condensation mocked me from inside my purse, declaring nothing was wrong.

Something inside most of us beats with a furious desire to be strong and capable – to be well. And it's a good thing! God made us for wholeness. But that same desire can be used against us when we are not well. We become ice-pack queens:

"You're sad?" An ice pack declares that *you won't feel like this forever.*

"You miss that?" *Well, on to bigger and better things.*

"They hurt your feelings?" *What doesn't kill us makes us stronger.*

"You're tired?" *From what?*

The people around me rarely hand out ice packs. I pick them up all on my own. However, I am slowly learning that God doesn't slap a cold compress over eyes brimming with tears. He doesn't hand out ice packs to quiet our complaints. I will never come to Him with something that feels broken and be told that I am fine.

I fear wallowing. I fight complaining. I'm guilty of both, but they drive me crazy. I'm finally learning that the remedy is not to suck it up and deal with it. The remedy is to take what is broken, what is tired, what feels dead into the presence of the one who binds up brokenness. He is the one who gives rest to the weary and breathes life back into what is dead.

In Luke 7:11-17, Jesus came upon a funeral procession for a widow's only son. She was not only grieving the death of her child, but also the death of her hopes, dreams, provision, and protection. I wonder if hopelessness threatened to consume her. I wonder if she rolled over to it or fought it with every bit of dignity she could muster. Did she sob loudly in the presence of others? Did she weep silently? Did she succumb to the grief? Did she stand in stubborn stoicism? She was weeping at the funeral. And Jesus, seeing her and feeling compassion, said, "Do not weep" (Luke 7:13). It sounds a little like an ice pack at first. And it would have been had those words not been spoken with the power of life pulsing through the God-Man. The next words Jesus spoke were to the dead son: "Young man, I say to you, arise!" (Luke 7:14). He did, and "Jesus gave him back to his mother" (Luke 7:15).

Tears of grief moved Jesus. He did not offer pleasant clichés or cover her pain with a frigid demand for faith. He came with compassion and moved with power. He spoke life back to the dead and returned hope to the one who had lost it.

I'm not naïve enough to think that His binding, healing, and life-giving are always so direct. Those we think we cannot live without die. When loss is real, so is grief. Dreams don't always come true, and when they don't, disappointment settles. Life, even when it's good, can still wear us down and burn us out. Denying those realities will never give us the strength and wholeness our spirits crave.

Instead, we bring our reality, raw and unpolished, to the feet of the one we are tempted to try to impress.

However big or small our burdens, we bring them to the feet of the one who can take them. And we trust Him with them. We trust Him with us. We lay down broken, and we tell Him where it hurts. And He comes right to us. He touches the coffin. He wipes the tears. He kneels beside us in our grief. While we fear the ice pack He might offer, we find His gentle power to heal the wound, speak life, whisper "arise," and be our strength as we do.

He doesn't just tell us that we're fine. Instead, He is faithful to hold us until we are well.

Respond

1. What does it mean to fake wellness? Do you think you are more prone to faking illness or faking wellness?
2. Are you carrying something (maybe someplace inside of you) that is dead, broken, or weary? What might it look like to bring it to Jesus?

Take some time now to sit in the presence of the Spirit of Christ, who meets you just as the Man of Christ met the grieving widow of Nain. Where do you need the Lord's comfort? What relationship or dream or desire within you has died a silent death? Is there an area where you need healing, physically or emotionally? Second Corinthians 1:3-5 says:

> *Blessed be the God and Father of our Lord Jesus Christ, the Father of mercies and the God of all comfort. He comforts us in all our affliction, so that we may be able to comfort those who are in any kind of affliction, through the comfort we ourselves receive from God. For just as the sufferings of Christ overflow to us, so also through Christ our comfort overflows. (2 Corinthians 1:3-5, CSB)*

The Lord can warm the stone-cold dead. And even when He doesn't, He is faithful to hold us tightly and comfort us through what we did not think we would survive.

Treasuring
Mary at the Birth of Christ
Luke 2:1-52

This morning began as most of my favorite mornings do. I took my cup of coffee into the living room and pulled my Bible and journal onto my lap. There is something comforting about their mass. Words are weightless until they are written and bound. Here I hold the pages of His Word and my words poured out for the other as a record of relationship, an evidence of history – something to hold onto when this always-present but often-intangible God is so hard to see.

I've filled countless journals with words that no one will ever read. No one. Ever. Because those words aren't for others' eyes. The Lord is faithful to meet me on the pages of His Scriptures, but He is also faithful to meet me on blank pages. Since I was old enough to put pen to paper, I've written and written and written, and He has faithfully read and read and read.

Secrets. Hopes. Dreams. Anger. A few lies. Guilt. Sadness. Fear. Excitement. Happiness. Disappointments. Wishes.

He has read stories I've made up. He has read words scrawled across the page in anger. He has read pages dotted with drops of tears – tiny memorials of disappointment and loss. He has read thoughts that trail off and are never finished, and He has read my deepest hopes and dreams – those I'm almost afraid to speak aloud. He has read the words I've later Sharpie-markered through, guarding the thoughts I'm sorry to have had.

He has revealed Himself to me there. And He has revealed *myself* to me there. In those secret, sacred places and moments and thoughts and emotions, those things tucked up close to my heart where only the gentle hand of God can reach, He has known me and made Himself known.

He has reached. He has tended. He has covered.

And here, in handwriting all my own, I have a written record of His faithfulness to me.

I've been thinking a lot about Mary, the mother of Jesus. Specifically, this verse: "But Mary treasured all these things, pondering them in her heart" (Luke 2:19).

The visit from an angel. The conversation with Joseph. The way her life shifted after that. The journey to Bethlehem. The birth in a stable. The visit from the shepherds, exhausted and surrounded by men she did not know. The lack of her mother and sisters and friends. Those tired moments in the dark of night, holding a baby close to her chest, thanking God He was hers, wondering where the girl she had been just a year ago had gone.

She treasured all those things, pondering them in her heart.

And I don't think Mary treasured them in her heart only because she had no one to tell. I think she knew the sweetness of moments that would cheapen if recounted. I think she knew the preciousness of thoughts that were only between herself and her Lord. I think she knew, as she stared into the freshly formed face of God in a way that no one else ever would, that the Savior meant to keep some moments between Himself and His mother.

So we read her story, but we do not read her fears or secrets, her joys or thoughts. We read an account of her life, but we do not read her journal. Because those things are none of our business. Mary kept some things just between her and her God. And do you know what I think? I think He did the same. I believe He honored her when He inspired His gospels by letting the unspoken things remain unspoken.

Some things need treasuring. We need to ponder them in our hearts. We need to lay them out before our Lord, knowing they will go no farther. Not because they are unworthy or unsightly but because they are so dear, precious, and deeply personal that no one but our Father would understand.

I'm not talking about secrets that need to see the light of day or wounds that need to be uncovered before another in order to be tended and healed. I'm not talking about those things we hide in shame or fear. I'm not talking about isolation.

I'm talking about those sweet and tender moments when we whisper or dream with only our Creator. I'm talking about what would be wasted without His presence. I'm talking about what might feel at first like loneliness but is actually the Savior pulling us aside, asking us our secrets, telling us His.

I'm there right now. I'm pondering things in my heart. I'm treasuring them. I'm wondering about some of them. There has been a little grieving and a little rejoicing and a whole lot of changing. And I don't want to tell you about it. But I want you to know that it's real.

And more than that, I want you to grab a cup of coffee and crawl up on your couch with just your God. What makes your heart beat faster with anticipation? What do you dream? What do you hope? What memories are so tender that you can't yet tell another? What moments are so dear that you want to keep them for yourself? What emotions are so raw that they confuse you? What passions run so deep that you're afraid to let them surface in the presence of another? Share them with Him. Ponder with Him.

And hear His gentle whisper in response: *I treasure these things too.*

There are some things that our faithful Father means to keep only between Himself and His daughter.

Respond

1. For me, these moments of pondering with the Lord are often done in writing, but the same may not be true for you. What do you do (or what could you do) to intentionally take time to ponder or treasure bits of your life with only the Lord? Do you like to go on walks with Him? Talk out loud to Him? Sit quietly, mulling things over with Him? Your Father delights when you share with Him.

2. What is the difference between the "treasuring" we observe in Mary's life and the negative "secret keeping" we might be tempted toward? (For further thought, consider Ephesians 5:11-16 and Matthew 6:1-21.)

One specific and intentional way to practice treasuring moments with the Lord is to bring our initial reactions to Him. Before sharing anything with another for the next seven days, take it to Jesus first. When you get good news, tell Him before you pick up the phone to tell another. When you hear something you aren't sure what to do with, lay it at the Lord's feet. When your heart aches with the longing that He knows so well, speak to Him before you confide in anyone else. Be intentional about it this week. Consider how you might carry this practice into the future when the week is over.

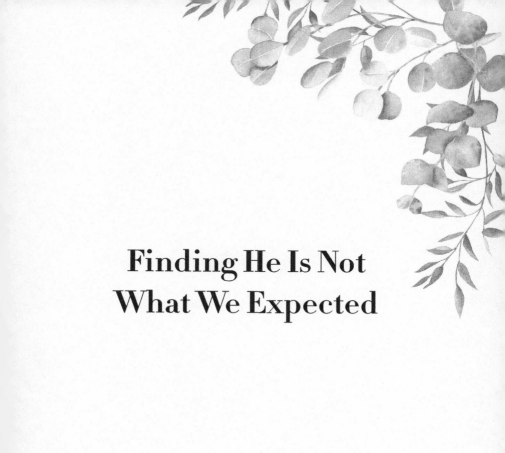

Finding He Is Not
What We Expected

Everything She Had to Live On

The Widow's Mite

Mark 12:41-44

She bit her lip and shook her fist a little to make sure her treasure was still there. She felt the two tiny coins click together against her sweaty palm and blinked back tears. Of acceptance? Of defeat? Of surrender? Of exhaustion? She took the last few steps quickly, completing the journey before she lost her nerve. She might have confessed that she wasn't sure if she was being faithful or careless, obedient or reckless. She wasn't sure if she was giving in or giving up.

She only knew that, clutching almost nothing, she also clutched her everything. Then she took a deep breath and threw her two half-cents into an offering box that rattled with the abundance of others. No one heard her treasure fall to the bottom of that box. No one heard her heart fall silent as a sob caught in her throat. Relief clamored against despair. Surrender felt a lot like defeat. Obedience felt a lot like failure.

She had brought everything. It looked like nothing.

Except to the Man that she did not see. He saw so clearly:

And [Jesus] called His disciples to Him and said to them, "Truly, I say to you, this poor widow has put in more than all those who are contributing to the offering box. For they all contributed out of their abundance, but she out of her poverty has put in everything she had, all she had to live on." (Mark 12:43-44)

All she had to live on. That's how much it cost. It cost everything she had. Even if it looked to the world like nothing.

I don't know how it feels to run out of resources or to throw your last penny into the well. But I know how it feels to run your fingers over that last fragile bit of self-assurance that we so often mistake for faith and then let it fall from your hands. I know how it feels to wonder if this is quitting or if this is surrender. I know how it feels to wonder if this is the kind of submission that leads to life or the kind of foolishness that leads to death.

When the well-meaning enthusiasts first tell you to give God your all, when they encourage you not to hold anything back and beckon you to go all in, it sounds exhilarating. It sounds like adventure. And that first handful of surrender feels like courage. The second handful feels like fearless obedience. The third handful. The fourth. There is swelling excitement. Confidence soars.

But when you're down to those last two copper coins that are only worth a penny? When you've reached the bottom of your treasure? When the last little bits of self-assurance click together in that sticky palm and mock all you thought you knew? When you wonder if you've made the whole thing up? In that moment?

Giving God your all loses all its glamour.

We scrape together and cling to those last remnants of resolve. We wonder what to do with them. We try to make them worth more than they are. We hide them. We polish them. We show them off. We pocket them. We wonder at how little they are and at how heavy. We wonder at our fatigue and weakness.

When did holding so little get to be so hard?

It is next to nothing, but it is too much to bear. Finally, our meager offering is too heavy to hold. And we get sick of looking at it. We hold that treasure tight once more and then throw it into the box alongside the apparent abundance of everyone else. It was all we had to live, but it was no life at all. And our hearts break because we have given all we have, and it still doesn't feel like enough. I said it to the Lord one Sunday. I wrote it down in my journal to make sure He understood: *"I'm very sorry,"* I said, *"but I have nothing left to give."*

And memories of others' words echoed back. Words of dear ones, of faithful ones, of honest ones. That she was afraid to hope. That she had nothing left to offer and was clinging to the last bit of what she'd always called faith because she didn't know where she'd be without it. That this wasn't what she'd expected or where she'd hoped her life would land when she'd whispered to God that she would follow Him.

We drop our eyes. Chin tucked to our chest. But the one that we've lost sight of sees it all.

She has put in everything she had, all she had to live on.

Jesus said it would cost everything to follow Him, but we're so surprised when it does.

I want this widow's story to have a pretty ending. I want Jesus to run after her. I want Him to pull gold and silver from the treasury to replace her copper coins. I want Him to fill her empty hands with plenty. It doesn't say that He did. Instead, He appears to have let her leave.

I glance down at my own fragile fingers that have held too tightly to everything I thought I could not live without, that have grabbed too quickly for everything I thought I wanted. And I turn my empty palms toward heaven.

I know this: It would have been wasted if it hadn't been for Him.

I wonder if God knows that empty hands will reach for His most quickly.

And He asks me if I know what's in His hand. The beginning of a smile plays on my lips because I can tell by His voice that He's already smiling. He is confident I'm going to like His answer. *"Remind me"*, I whisper back to Him.

"You are," He says. (See Isaiah 49:16 and John 10:29.)

Our hands may be empty. But we are safely held in His.

Respond

1. Have you ever faced a decision or circumstance that caused you to feel like you weren't sure whether you were being faithful or foolish? When?

2. What are you tempted to hold onto in your own strength rather surrender and entrust it back to the One who gave it to you?

I once heard singer and songwriter Christy Nockels describe an idol as "anything we're holding onto just in case Jesus doesn't come through."

Ask the Lord to bring to mind anything you are clinging onto "just in case Jesus doesn't come through." Is there some action you need to take to surrender those things to Jesus? Or is He asking you to adjust the position of your heart as you surrender those things to Him? Name the things before Him and ask Him to sort through them with you. What does it look like to surrender them to the Lord and allow Jesus to hold them as He holds you? He is faithful, and we can trust Him even with the things we are tempted to cling to.

Misplaced Hope

The Mother of James and John

Matthew 20:20-28

We throw the word "hope" around like sprinkles or confetti, as though it's weightless or decorative rather than foundational.

We know we need faith. We get that love is important. But hope? What even is hope? Is it the childish notion that everything will magically be okay even when it is not? Is it the naïve idea that wishing for something might make it so? Is it the power of positive thinking?

I have been reading through the Bible in a translation different from the one I'm used to. Throughout the Psalms in the Christian Standard Bible, the psalmists' words about hope are translated as "putting" our hope (emphasis mine):

> "Be strong, and let your heart be courageous, all you who *put* your hope in the LORD." (Psalm 31:24, CSB)

> "May your faithful love rest on us, Lord, for we *put* our hope in you." (Psalm 33:22, CSB)

> "*Put* your hope in God, for I will still praise Him." (Psalm 42:11, CSB)

"I will *put* my hope in your name, for it is good." (Psalm 52:9, CSB)

In other translations, the same idea is presented as to "wait on the Lord" or to "hope in Him," but there is something powerful about the image of *putting* our hope.

Hebrews 6:19 describes hope as an "anchor of our soul." Hope is far weightier than the wishful thinking we've equated with it. The "hope" that Scripture speaks of is better defined as "joyful and confident expectation."[2]

We are responsible for our expectations and hope. We *set* our expectations. We *put* our hope. A friend once said she imagined this *putting* of our hope as clipping a carabiner while rock climbing: You choose where to attach it, and you'd better be sure it's attached somewhere securely before you scale the jagged cliff.

When we set our expectations on something that is not guaranteed, we risk disappointment. When we put our hope in something that doesn't come to pass, we feel the sting of loss.

This is bad news because we can misplace our hope. It's good news because we can *re*-place our hope. We can hook it to something more secure.

James and John were two of Jesus' disciples. Toward the end of Jesus' earthly ministry, their mother approached Jesus, looking for security. She was searching for a sturdy place to hook her hope. She was seeking a steady and sure anchor for her soul. She was asking Jesus to grant her desires:

And [Jesus] said to her, "What do you want?" She said to him, "Say that these two sons of mine are to sit, one at your right hand and one at your left, in your kingdom."

2 "G1680 - elpis - Strong's Greek Lexicon (nasb95)." Blue Letter Bible. Accessed 11 Nov, 2022. https://www.blueletterbible.org/lexicon/g1680/nasb95/tr/0-1/.

Jesus answered, "You do not know what you are asking. Are you able to drink the cup that I am to drink?" They said to him, "We are able."

He said to them, "You will drink my cup, but to sit at my right hand and at my left is not mine to grant, but it is for those for whom it has been prepared by my Father." (Matthew 20:21-23)

You do not know what you are asking.
You do not realize where you are setting your expectation.
You do not recognize where you are putting your hope.

Some Bibles even translate her words as "*Promise* that these two sons of mine may sit, one on your right and the other on your left, in your kingdom" (Matthew 20:21, CSB, emphasis mine).

How often have we asked the same? Perhaps not for a throne beside Jesus, but for a guarantee that He will grant our wishes.

Promise me health. Promise me a husband. Promise me ease for my family. Promise me health. Promise me the dream job. Promise me success. Promise me.

Promise. Promise. Promise.

Then we obligate Jesus to keep a promise He's never made. We think we know the better way. We ask for an outcome and tell Him He's failed if He delivers anything else. We hope for one thing, and our despair turns to disillusionment when He does not deliver what He never said He'd give.

Our expectations go unmet, and our faith buckles as our hope deflates.

But our hope was never meant to be so fragile.

We weren't promised ease. We weren't promised husbands. We weren't promised dream jobs or quick answers or bodies that never fail.

We've tied our hope to a thousand different dreams, and wishes don't always come true.

I don't mean to sound callous. I get it. These losses and disappointments will always cut deep, but I'm also worried about us. Because if, along with earthly losses, we lose our faith in God, we really *will* be without hope in this world. If we measure God's faithfulness by what we *wish* He'd do, our expectations will forever go unmet, and our hope will waiver.

We will not find God faithful if we measure His faithfulness against promises He hasn't made.

He hasn't promised us everything we want, but He has promised us His presence. He has promised us His Spirit. He has promised us peace, joy, rest, and *life* right here in the middle of a world still ravaged by sin and death.

Right here, where bodies fail and dreams die and families shatter, God still dwells with us.

The mother of James and John wanted to know who would sit beside the King of Kings; she wanted her sons to have secured seats next to Him. Here was a woman who could approach the Man of Christ. She could walk up beside Him on the road. She had ease of access to Him because of her sons' relationship with Him.

As we come up beside them on this dusty road, what amazes me is that even though Jesus didn't grant her request, He also didn't send her away. He didn't promise her that her sons would sit enthroned beside Him, but He didn't chastise her for approaching Him with her desires.

Instead, He spoke straight to the heart of her need: "The Son of Man did not come to be served, but to serve, and to give His life as a ransom for many" (Matthew 20:28).

He came to do all that was necessary to welcome her into His presence.

He came that she might continue to come to Him.

He came that we might also boldly approach this Man whose worth we'll never rival.

He did not come to offer us a throne. He came to invite us to approach His.

I am tempted to think that Jesus-on-earth was somehow more approachable than Jesus-in-heaven. I am tempted to think that I'd have approached Him more boldly as He sat beside the sea than I can now that He is seated upon a throne. I am tempted to ask for a guarantee that I'm welcome. I am tempted to try to secure a promise that He didn't make.

And in my mind's eye, Jesus rubs His thumb against His palm, tracing the visible reminders of His faithfulness.

The miracle isn't what we are able to compel Jesus to do for us. The miracle is that we can approach Him at all! The miracle is that God-Made-Flesh walked among His people, and one mother felt comfortable enough to ask Him to make her a promise. The miracle is that we get to come before the one seated on the throne and boldly ask Him for what we need and desire (Hebrews 4:16).

The miracle is that the King of Kings, the only one worthy of the throne we sometimes seek for ourselves, is still Immanuel, God with us.

The miracle is that He holds out His nail-pierced hands and invites us to secure our ropes of hope right there to His palm.

The miracle is that we are invited to find our hope in His presence – to find Him faithful far beyond the promises we've tried to make Him keep.

Respond

1. How do you understand the difference between biblical hope and how we use "hope" in our everyday conversations?
2. What promises have you asked God to make where He has not assured you of the outcome? Are you measuring His faithfulness against His willingness to do what He has not promised He will do?

Think about where your hope is shaking. What perceived outcome do you think would have to happen? What promise would Jesus have to make to you in order for you to feel secure? Can you, like James' and John's mother, admit to Him what your wishes are? And then, can you ask Him to show you how to secure your hope to Him – to the promises He has made rather than the circumstances that you are asking for?

If You Had Been Here

Mary and Martha at their Brother's Death

John 11:1-46

Mary knew Jesus. She knew what it was to sit in His presence and hang on His every word (Luke 10:38-42). She knew that He loved and cared for her. And so, when her brother fell ill, she and her sister, Martha, called for the Teacher that they knew was the Healer: "Lord, he whom You love is ill" (John 11:3).

Did Mary begin to wait, confident of her Lord's imminent arrival? When did her confidence give way to confusion? When did her patience fade to heartache? When did her hope crash blindly into disappointment?

Jesus delayed until her brother's failing body succumbed to death. Not only was their brother gone, Jesus hadn't come. Hope waned as death won, and grief landed heavy on the hearts of the hopeful.

I wonder if grief crumpled Mary in the same place she'd once knelt at the Lord's feet. I wonder if she stared hard at the place where He had once sat in her home. Did she will herself to remember and to believe it had been real? I'd wager that she lost more than her brother that day. I'd be willing to bet that, at least for a moment, she also lost her confidence in the one she knew could have healed him.

Here's the thing. We can *know* Jesus. We can be absolutely certain that He is good. We can be perfectly confident that He is near. We can know the joy of sitting at His feet. We can have faith that looks to Him first when our brother falls ill – when the relationship, job, or dream starts failing.

And we can still feel the sting of loss when He doesn't respond as we expected.

I wonder if you have felt that loss. I don't know what might have dropped you to the ground – fear, illness, grief, guilt, shame. I don't know if someone did something to you or if you think you brought it on yourself. But I know that it hurts to lose the confidence you once had in your God.

Where do you go with all that pain? What do you do with all that confusion?

Four days after their brother's body was laid in the grave, the sisters got word that Jesus was coming. Martha, always a picture of practicality (say what you will about her busyness, she was also a woman of fortitude and determination), went to Jesus when she heard He was on His way. I don't know, but I imagine she wiped the tears from her cheeks, took a deep breath, squared her shoulders, and maintained her composure as she spoke. She professed her grief but summoned her faith. She stood there and reasoned through a conversation with Jesus. She declared her belief in Him as the Christ, the Son of God. She fought to stand strong in the presence of the Savior.

Not Mary. Mary didn't move until her sister returned to her "saying in private, 'The Teacher is here and is calling for you'" (John 11:28).

I know what it is to sit paralyzed in a place where you once knew the Lord. I know what it is to silence your prayers rather than risk feeling ignored. I know what it is to resist hope for fear of disappointment.

And I know the sweetness of a sister who will drop to her knees beside you and whisper, "The Teacher is here and is calling for you" (John 11:28). *Our Lord is near. He hasn't left you all alone. He hasn't forgotten you. He didn't ignore you. I have been with Him, and He still loves you. You are still so welcome at His feet.*

You may have lost sight of Him, but He has never taken His eyes off you.

It was only after Martha spoke her invitation that Mary went to Jesus. When she rose, I doubt she checked her face in the mirror. I doubt she tucked loose hair behind her ear. I imagine she ran, breath catching in angry sobs. No composure here. No reasoning. No profession of faith. Or was there? When she got to her Lord, she fell at His feet, exhausted and angry and desperately sad. "If you had been here, my brother would not have died" (John 11:32).

Perhaps this was faith at its truest.

We look around this world, so full of pain and hurt and death, and we say to the Lord, "Surely You could make this turn out differently." We land in a heap at His feet and, through sobs, declare what feels like doubt, what looks like hopelessness, what sounds like despair. But what hurts the most as we choke out "if You had been here" is that stubborn hope refuses to stop fluttering against our raw and aching hearts. There is faith that will not die. There is an enduring belief in God's goodness and power that will not let us settle comfortably into a world ravaged by sin and death.

Mary didn't put elegant words on her faith that day. And who can blame her? She finally threw herself at the feet of Christ, the one she adored, and she wept. She confessed a faith of brokenness but a faith nonetheless: "Lord, if You had been here" (John 11:32). She knew the Lord was good and able and that He would not stand idly by.

Here is where the story gets wild. Mary's grief moved Him. He asked where Lazarus had been laid, and then two words of Scripture shatter any doubt of Jesus' humanity: "Jesus wept" (John 11:35). What must that sound have been like in Mary's ears?

We come to Jesus confused and broken by things we have seen that we cannot understand. We come to Him angry about the things He could have but did not change. We come to Him desperate for intervention. We come to Him furious and exhausted and certain we've been betrayed. We come to Him sure that this world is not how it should be.

The important thing, though, is that we *come* to Him.

Might it be that He does not chastise us for doubts or lack of faith in those moments? Could it be that He does not judge us for disbelief? Might His words not be words of anger or even correction? Perhaps the whisper we'd hear as His tears mingle with our own is this – *"You are right, child. This is not the way that it was meant to be."*

Might He be glad that we've realized it? Might He weep with us? Might the very brokenness of our own hearts reflect His?

Sometimes we need a moment to weep in the presence of a Savior who weeps with us. Sometimes we need a minute at His feet to confess a broken faith in a perfect God – to hurt and to know we are held.

In case you sit paralyzed, afraid to hope that He might be near, let mine be the voice of a sister reminding you that *the Teacher is here and is calling for you. You are so welcome at His feet.* I whisper it with a heart tendered by my own recent fear that it might not be true. I whisper it with a heart relieved to rest again in the presence of the one who has been here all along.

Bring your fear, doubt, and disappointment. Bring your anger, failure, and shame.

Fall at the feet of the one whose love is perfect even when our faith is not.

In the next moment, we see Jesus calling Lazarus forth from the tomb. Mary got her miracle; Martha received back her dead. Jesus set their wrong right. And so we pray. We ask Him to raise the dead. We beg Him to remedy injustice. We cry out for Christ to return and set right all that has spiraled into chaos since that serpent slithered his way into the mind of man. We wait and hope. We pray and trust.

I believe in miracles. I believe in captives set free and dead raised. I believe the lame will walk, and the deaf will hear. I know our God can do it! And, if I am really honest, it puzzles me when He does not.

But I pray for faith as stubborn as Mary's. I pray for hope that refuses to die – *if You had been here, if You had moved* – because inherent in that outcry is the belief that He is able and good. And that He does not – that He *can*not – stand idly by. Even if we lack for a miracle, may it never be mistaken for a lack of the presence of God.

When our hearts break and our fury rises, may love drive us to the feet of our Lord. When we cry out, may it be to the one who always hears. When we weep, may we know we move the very heart of God.

Sometimes heartbreak is evidence of faith.

Respond

1. When have you been disappointed by an outcome different from the one you trusted God for? How did it affect your faith and your relationship with the Lord?
2. Is there any disappointment, confusion, or heartache you have hesitated to lay at Jesus' feet? Why do you carry it? What makes you hesitate to give it to Him?

Spend some time in the presence of Christ. Lay down or curl up or stand at His feet and confess to Him the things that have kept you from Him – those heartbreaks and disappointments and confusing circumstances that have made you wonder where He was. He can handle it. He can hold it. You don't have to bear that burden any longer. Start your prayer, "If You had been here, Jesus…" and let Him meet you right in the middle of the pain.

I don't want us to walk away from Him with the same hurt and disappointment that we approached Him with. To do so would be to miss an invitation from the very heart of God. Jesus met Mary in her pain; He wept beside her. But He also restored her faith and hope in Him. Would you be willing to hand Him your unmet expectations and the pain associated with them? Imagine packaging it all up in the words you've just shared with Him and then handing it over to Him. As you do, ask Him what He has in exchange for the hurt and pain you've carried. Write down what you sense He is giving you in place of that disillusionment.

Bearing the Barren

Elizabeth

Luke 1:1-25

Zechariah and Elizabeth walked blamelessly before the Lord. They obeyed Him as best they knew how. They sought and served Him according to His commands. But the Scripture tells us, "They had no child because Elizabeth was barren" (Luke 1:7) In a world where children were viewed as evidence of God's blessing, these two faithful followers of God were unable to conceive. What was this holy couple to make of their empty home?

What did they make of the quiet where they had hoped for cries?

What did they make of silent nights when they had hoped for midnight feedings?

What did they make of the lack of God's movement in their lives?

In a world of productivity and performance, what do *we* make of the stillness and the promises that seem to have stalled? What do we make of the months when the Father's movement is nearly imperceptible?

What do we do in those seasons with a verse like this one: "It is to the Father's glory that you bear much fruit" (John 15:8)?

What about the winters when your branches lay bare, and the Father's pruning strips you of all you thought you knew?

What about the winters when you *want* to bear fruit, but it's all you can do to rest on the wings of the One who bears *you*?

My gardening habit began years ago with two plants on my porch, and they froze one winter. Where life had flourished, mere stalks remained. I thought they had died, but when I went to pull them from their pots, the branches weren't as brittle as they looked. Hidden life still coursed inside. So I trimmed them back and left those ugly, stalky things outside.

Perhaps you know the feeling. Stripped and bare. Little to offer. Little to show. No easy answers to others' questions. No one-liners to summarize your purpose. No evidence of fruitfulness.

Just a nagging thought that is half-hope and half-hurt: If it is to the Father's glory that I bear much fruit, what does He make of our barrenness?

One afternoon that spring, I walked outside and was surprised to see that fresh leaves had sprouted on those plants that looked so dead.

No, it wasn't fruit. But it was evidence of life. The hope of it catches again in my throat.

Elizabeth knew the hesitant hope that accompanies those first signs of life. She had been barren so long that she must have been shocked to find herself with child. It doesn't surprise me that she kept herself hidden for the first five months of her pregnancy. I think of the comfort that nausea must have been and the thrill of the first flutter-kicks of life within. I think of the joy and the hope and the excitement and how fragile she must have felt. Content. Peaceful. Tendered to rest in the presence of God alone.

It had always been to the Father's glory that she bear a son. Even in those seasons of childlessness.

I do not know the way a child moves against your ribs, but I know that new life's flutters are felt most fully in the stillness. I know that the first and fleeting sense of God's movement after a season of doubt awakens a tender hope. I know how fragile faith feels and how hard it is to wrap words around the renewed promise of a few green leaves on an otherwise barren stalk. I know it's sometimes sweeter to be alone with the one who has spoken than to speak His words aloud, even to those dearest to you.

I know that hiding *from* God will isolate you. I know that hiding *in* God can save you.

It is to the Father's glory that we bear much fruit.

But there are seasons of pruning when the Father takes blade to branch and leaves us broken but not abandoned. There are months when the only evidence of life is that our stalks are not as brittle as they look, when life beneath the surface is the only life we know, when roots search through soil to cling to God alone.

The Father tends those first green leaves of growth, and we stare in wonder at the life we would not have noticed if we had not been laid so bare.

Hope flutters, and faith finds its footing while we hide away with our Maker and whisper with the awe of Elizabeth, "Thus the Lord has done for me in the days when He looked on me" (Luke 1:25).

And we remember that the sweetness of the fruit was never about the efficiency of the production and always about the presence of the one in whom we dwell: "Whoever abides in Me and I in him, he it is that bears much fruit" (John 15:5).

Yes, it is to the Father's glory that we bear much fruit. But it is the Father who has born us all along:

"You yourselves have seen what I did to the Egyptians, and how I bore you on eagles' wings and brought you to myself." (Exodus 19:4)

The Lord bore the Israelites and brought them our of their captivity to the land that He had promised to them. Generations after the exodus, the same God who had born the Israelites out of Egypt looked upon Elizabeth, and He bore the barren woman until she bore a son.

So today, we can trust the Vinedresser with His blade. We can trust Him with our barren stalks and our tender leaves. It is to His glory that we bear much fruit.

In this season, we may not bear the fruit we thought we would, but we can trust our Father even in those seasons when He bears us in our barrenness to draw us to Himself.

Respond

1. Are you currently or have you ever been in a season of pruning that feels fruitless? (See John 15:1-11.) What kind of branches does the Father prune, and what is His goal in the pruning according to John 15:2?

2. What is the difference between hiding *in* God and hiding *from* God? How does each play out in your own life? For example, when I am hiding *in* God, I value and crave time alone with Him, but I also enjoy community and am more patient and kind to those around me. When I am hiding *from* God, I surround myself with people to avoid being alone, but I'm irritable and impatient most of the time because I'm not engaging the Lord or His people in healthy ways.

The reminder of John 15:1-11 is to abide in Christ. Regardless of the season you're in (whether it's one of fruitfulness or pruning), take heart! Ask Him to give you eyes to see the ways that He is bringing you to Himself. Ask Him to show you what it means to abide in Him. Sometimes the long and lonely times when we feel the least productive turn out to be seasons of solitude, where God brought us to Himself. Sometimes those moments between the two of you become the sweetest milestones along your journey. Ask Him to teach you to treasure the solitude (in whatever form it comes) during the current season of your life. Practice abiding in Him even in the still, small, solitary moments of your day.

Faith at Rest

The Mother of Jesus at the Cross

John 19:16-27

Here are a few fun facts to get us started:

> The gravitational pull of the earth is 9.8 meters per second squared.

> A tripod cannot wobble. It can fall over, but it cannot be unsteady like a four-legged stool or table can.

> Ants are, proportionally speaking, stronger than you. They can carry 10-50 times their body weight.

The facts above are true regardless of whether you believe me or understand why they are true. Your belief or disbelief does nothing to affect the truth.

And yet, we approach belief in God as though so much is riding on us. We look to God and think that His faithfulness is somehow dependent on our ability to have faith.

There is a holy invitation to *believe* Him, but I wonder if faith may have gotten twisted along the way.

I do not intend to demean or belittle belief. It is huge. But what if we approach the Lord differently this time?

What if we don't come with our hands clasped around the things we believe? What if we don't look down to rifle through the faith we clutch? What if, instead, we come with arms reaching up like a child, looking to the one we believe in? What if we come with empty hands reaching for the hand of the one whose grip is sure (John 10:28-29)?

What if we don't come demanding answers but, instead, we ask that His Spirit might build in us a faith beyond our comprehension?

Mary, the mother of Jesus, beheld the face of God in a way that no one else will. She looked into the puckered lips of her newborn, and she saw the mouth that had spoken the world into being. She wiped the blood that would be shed for us from the skinned knee of her toddler. He spoke His first, rambling words, and Mary heard the voice of God. She held the hands that hold the world.

God came down as a fragile child, and His mother watched Him grow into a man.

What must it have been like to be the girl who was blessed to believe all that the Lord had spoken to her (Luke 1:45)? To become the mother of God and to treasure up all those things in her heart (Luke 2:19)? To raise the Son of God, and to ponder all that she saw of Him (Luke 2:51)?

To stare into the face of God and find her faith not in the things she could explain or understand but in the one she beheld.

God is good, and He does good. God is faithful. He is near. He is holy. He is powerful. But His ways are not our ways, and sometimes we're left wondering in His wake.

Sometimes we're left reeling to sort through what we thought we knew.

Even Jesus' mother found herself weeping at the foot of the cross. She watched her beaten and battered son die the most painful of deaths. She knew what she knew of her God, but I wonder if she wondered about all the reasons for her son's suffering.

Sometimes our faith falters, and we wonder if the Faithful One has faltered too.

Hopefully, in those moments when we cannot make sense of our faith, we will remember to "be still and know that He is God" (Psalm 46:10). Hopefully, we will remember that He isn't made secure by our faith, that He is all that He regardless of what we believe.

Just like gravity. And tripods. And the strength of ants.

Might that give us the comfort we need to catch our breaths and sit in the questions *with* the Lord? Not demanding answers but just looking up at Him.

What if Mary's faith wasn't evident in her ability to understand the cross or even in her ability to accept it? What if her faith was most apparent in the simple act of shifting her gaze toward the one she knew and loved even in the midst of what she could not comprehend?

What if our faith isn't our ability to conjure up the right feelings or recite the right facts? What if our faith is the simple act of lifting our eyes to Our God?

What if faith looks more like trust and less like understanding?

But we will only trust one that we know. We will only trust one who is faithful. And our Faithful Father knows that.

What if we come expectant, not searching for our faith but searching instead for the Faithful One?

What if, regardless of the mess or the beauty in which we find ourselves, we shift our eyes heavenward and believe?

Not because our faith is mighty. But because our God is.

Respond

1. How would you describe the difference between clinging to our own "faith" and resting in the faithfulness of God?
2. What have you seen or experienced of God that allows you to trust Him? How has His faithfulness built your faith? On the other hand, when has your own faith faltered? How has it affected your relationship with the Lord?

Sometimes we need to lay down our need to "figure it all out" in order to find real peace and rest in God. Fix your eyes on Jesus and let Him build your faith by showing you His faithfulness. Tell the Lord about the things you don't understand. Don't worry about figuring them out or explaining them away. Instead, look up to your God in the midst of them just as Mary looked up to her son on the cross.

A Feast of Crumbs

The Canaanite Woman

Matthew 15:21-28

This woman's encounter with Jesus is a puzzle to me. I've skipped and ignored it. I've thought about leaving it out altogether. I do not know what to do with it because I'm a little bit offended for this Gentile woman and her apparent humiliation by the one who'd welcomed everybody else.

But then, she also got what she wanted: Jesus healed her daughter and praised her faith. While I cringe at Jesus' initial reception of her, I also envy her results. Some of us who know we are welcome in the presence of God may be wondering why we don't get what we want while this woman did! Clearly, there is more going on here than is immediately evident to our western ways.

The Canaanite woman in this passage was a Gentile; she was not an Israelite descended from the chosen line of Abraham to whom God had made many promises. I am also a Gentile woman. So this story gives me pause, causes me to stare squarely into the face of Jesus and ask Him whether it's true that He has indeed come for the whole world.

Why the favoritism? Why the prejudice? Is that what's going on here?

I want to pull this woman aside and assure her that Jesus didn't mean it the way it sounded. (And then I want to pull Jesus aside and let Him know how it sounded!)

To be honest, I'm not exactly sure what He *did* mean by His reception of her.

The Canaanites had descended from Noah's son Ham and grandson Canaan. When Ham disrespected and mocked his father Noah for his drunkenness, Noah's response was to curse Ham's offspring through Canaan (Genesis 9:25). This woman, a Canaanite, was part of that group of people – the cursed group of people that God had commanded the Israelites to drive out of the Promised Land when they entered it under the leadership of Joshua (Joshua 3:10).

It's a miracle that this woman dared approach Christ at all. She knew exactly who He was! She called Him the "Son of David" (Matthew 15:22), a reference to Jesus' lineage through King David as the promised Messiah.

Unlike many of the Pharisees and devout Jews who questioned Jesus' authority, doubted His claims, and denied His power, this woman, who had no genealogical entitlement to the promises of God, trusted His goodness in a way that I can hardly fathom.

His disciples wanted to send her away, but she came directly to the man who held her only hope. She knelt before Him. She begged for His help. (Matthew 15:23-25)

In response, Jesus compared her to a dog asking for the bread intended for the children (Matthew 15:26).

And, in a display of astounding faith, she didn't walk away.

Even just the crumbs from your table would be enough, she implored. *I'll take whatever you can offer.*

I want to make excuses for Jesus' apparent rudeness to her. I want to reassure her that this is just a misunderstanding, that He doesn't mean what He seems to have said. I want to remind her of His kindness. I want to fast-forward her to the cross and read her John 3:16 and try to explain to her that Jesus really has come for the whole world! I would speak too fast and make no sense in my rush to preserve her surely wavering faith.

But instead, I can almost sense her calm smile and gentle hand of reassurance.

She trusts this man far more fully than I do. She knows something of His kindness and His goodness that I have failed to see.

She hasn't come to test Him. She hasn't come to see if He will prove that He is who He says He is. She has come because she *knows* He is who He says He is; He is her daughter's only hope.

She would take whatever He offered. She would receive whatever He could spare.

She knew that even the scraps from His table would satisfy the starving.

In my estimation, she received far more than crumbs. She got exactly what she asked for: "Then Jesus answered her, 'O woman, great is your faith! Be it done for you as you desire.' And her daughter was healed instantly" (Matthew 15:28).

Why did she get what she wanted? Why do I so often walk away unsatisfied?

I don't know. *Can I say that here?*

I've watched children go unhealed and marriages dissolve. I've watched mental illness gnaw through relationships and healthy bodies eaten by disease. I've watched, and I've wondered, and I've nearly walked away.

But I'm still drawn to this man, to His Spirit, because I know who He is even when I don't understand what He's doing. He does not always do what I expect, so I long for the faith of this Canaanite woman who refused to walk away.

I don't fully understand the nuances of their exchange, but I'll let her story speak of the Son of David's goodness. I'll let her staying and her kneeling testify of His kindness.

She would rather receive His scraps than walk away. She would take whatever He would offer because she knew, perhaps in a way I still can't quite fathom, that He was trustworthy.

And so the next time I feel rejected, the next time His answer is delayed, the next time I feel unfavored and unseen, I'll remember that He is still the Son of David. He is still the Savior of the world. He is still the one that He has always been.

We can still trust Him.

Perhaps her bold confidence will help me stay even when the Lord is not what I expected.

Respond

1. Have you ever feared that you were unwelcomed by Jesus? If so, how does this woman's story encourage you?

2. When have you been confused by something that you did not receive? How did that affect your faith and trust in Jesus? How did you make sense of His failure to act on your behalf?

I'm going to ask something of you here that I'm also asking of myself. Make a list of times that Jesus wasn't the way you expected Him to be, of times when He didn't act the way you wanted Him to. Then I want you to revisit those times with Him and ask Him what conclusions you drew from that experience. Sometimes, when our expectations go unmet, we draw false conclusions about ourselves or our God in our attempt to understand something that confuses us. As He brings to mind any conclusions you drew from your experience, compare that conclusion against what you know of Him. Ask Him to replace your misunderstandings with His truth. Ask Him to remind you of who He is.

God's identity does not change because we misunderstand Him or believe Him to be something He is not. But our faith and our relationship with Him will suffer if we hold onto our false conclusions rather than allowing Him to replace those misunderstandings with the truth of who He is. I pray we would be women willing to live confident in who God is, even when we must confess that we don't always understand His ways.

Exposed
The Adulterous Woman
John 8:1-11

I wonder how she felt standing there, alone and exposed before the people who would condemn her and before the only one who had every right to do so. I wonder if she was hardened to the stares or if her eyes welled with tears. I wonder if she felt like a stranger in her own life. I wonder if guilt settled, heavy in the pit of her stomach, or if anger boiled over, silencing conviction.

I wonder if she looked up, pleading, to Christ or if she lowered her eyes from His.

I imagine she might have been staring at the dirt under His feet because that is where His eyes went, too. He knelt where she had fixed her gaze and wrote with His finger on the ground. Sometimes the dirt is the only thing familiar. The wind whipped it into her eyes, and it stuck to her exposed flesh.

Caught. Guilty. Without excuse. Heart drops. Stomach turns. Knees weaken. Palms sweat.

I hate that feeling. I hate that it's familiar. I wish I could defend myself. I wish I could blame someone else. I wish I had an answer. But I don't. My voice catches in my tightening throat – *I was wrong, and perhaps even worse, I was found out.*

Was Jesus' writing enough of a diversion that this woman felt herself gasp for the breath she had been holding? Her accusers still gripped the stones they held. Did their voices ring in her ears, or did the pounding of her own heart muffle them? Then Jesus stood, and He spoke: "Let him who is without sin be the first to throw a stone at her" (John 8:7).

And then He knelt again in the dirt.

One by one, the stones fell until they were the only thing left of the accusers who had stood before her. Until it was just the two of them – just Jesus and this woman named only by her sin. There was no one left for her to face except the Lord Himself. She stood before Him, and He, wiping the dust from his fingertips, straightened to look at her as He asked, "Has no one condemned you?" (John 8:10).

"No one, Lord" (John 8:11).

No one. No one stands to threaten when the Lord bends to protect. No one stays to slaughter when He speaks to preserve. No one is left to condemn when the Savior Himself has knelt in the dirt of our earth, written new words into the filth of our stains, and touched the ground where our accusers stood.

"Neither do I condemn you; go, and from now on sin no more" (John 8:11).

That moment is when I would have broken. That moment when Jesus declares that all my flailing and faltering is not my future. That moment when standing accurately accused before Him, He lifts my chin so that my gaze meets His, and He whispers that He does not mean for me to stand covered in the filth of this earth. That moment when He shows me His dust-covered fingers and His nail-pierced hands, and He says with a voice of the gentlest strength: "It is finished" (John 19:30).

That moment. That is when my stubborn stoicism softens.

Yes, *it* is finished.

But, oh Lord, *I* am not.

In every graduation season, a familiar Bible verse floats around: "I am sure of this, that He who began a good work in you will bring it to completion at the day of Jesus Christ" (Philippians 1:6). I remember the hope that verse held years ago at my high school graduation. I was moving toward some beautiful goal – this thing of *completion*. I didn't know what it looked like, and I wasn't sure what it meant, but I was confident of my future arrival. This esoteric destination was the cry of my heart: *complete*. I wanted to know I would one day be a finished work.

All these years later, I just want to know that He's still working. I just want to know that this is not the time He'll leave me standing alone in the dust of choices I wish I had not made. I just want to know that He hasn't given up on me. And all these years later, He still answers with the same kind conviction: "Go, and from now on sin no more" (John 8:11).

Yes, I hear the correction and discipline in His voice. I hear the firmness and weep at the sound of it. Because it means He still finds me worthy of molding. He still looks at me and sees someone worth shaping. I have not successfully flung myself from His arms. He still sees. He still cares. He still works. He still moves to make me more like Him.

He still says to go from here, and I want to tell Him: *No! Let me stay here. I'll mess this up again. I will go and sin some more, just like last time.*

But the echo of His promise soothes my worry. Maybe this is what He meant when He said, "I tell you the truth: it is to your advantage that I go away, for if I do not go away, the Helper will not come to you. But if I go, I will send him to you" (John 16:7).

I need more than His forgiveness. I need the power of His Spirit within me to transform my desires.

I'm reminded of a quote from Ted Dekker's novel, *A.D. 30*, in which a fictional woman encounters the Man of Christ. While separated from Him, she recalls her experience:

> I tried to hold onto my surreal encounter with [Jesus] in Capernaum. But His power was not with me in my cell, and though I tried to follow His teaching to release fear, I could not find a way to shift my mind. With each passing day, my memory of Him seemed to fade.[3]

We need far more than understanding or a memory of who Jesus once was, of all He did as He walked in this world. We need to be filled with the power of His Spirit, which He delights to give.

He still kneels in the dust that swirls around my feet.

He still speaks to remind me that this dust is not my home.

He still pours out His Spirit that my heart might be made whole, that I might walk away changed, that I might really overcome the sin that has entangled – not in my own strength, but in His. (Romans 8:11)

His kindness is never what I expected. It is always more than I dared to hope.

---

3 Dekker, Ted. *A.D. 30*. New York, NY: Center Street, 2014. Page 279.

Respond

1. Think back to the last time you were caught in the wrongness of your own choices. How did it feel? How did you respond? What did you do when you realized the gravity of your mistake, of your sin?
2. When we have done wrong, we are often tempted to make excuses rather than seek forgiveness. What sin have you recently tried to excuse rather than confess it to the Lord?

I want you to feel the weight of your sin. Picture yourself standing as exposed as the woman in John 8. She's not been wrongfully accused. She's been caught red-handed. And often, so have we. Let yourself feel the gravity of it. Now imagine Jesus standing there with you. He kneels, and the eyes of everyone shift from you to the Savior as He writes in the dust that swirls around your feet. Confess the sin you've tried to hide. He writes your sin in the sand, but He has engraved His love in the palm of His hand. See Him as He stands. Hear Him as He speaks: "I do not condemn you" (Romans 8:1). Feel the weight of your sin. See that the significance of His sacrifice far outweighs it.

"Go, and sin no more" (John 8:11), He says, and you feel the defeat of knowing you will indeed sin again. But the Savior of the world, who knelt in the dust, has sent His Spirit to dwell within you. Open your hands to Him, acknowledge your desperate need of His empowering presence; ask Him to fill you fresh with His Spirit so that you might live the life He died to secure for you (Romans 8:11).

Missing Jesus
Mary
Luke 2:41-52

My brother got lost at Disney World when we were little. It was pretty traumatic – for us, not for Hunter. He had decided to visit the playground, so he climbed out of his stroller and had a great time during the brief eternity we searched for him.

My grandmother found him. He was waving at her from the top of a slide. My parents were that grateful kind of angry – the kind that hugs and holds and also wants to pummel the one we'd lost.

Furious relief.

I imagine Mary (the mother of Jesus) might have felt the same furious relief after she'd lost Jesus.

Mary didn't find Jesus waving from the top of the playground. Instead, she found Him sitting calmly in the Temple. "Why were you looking for Me? Did you not know that I must be in My Father's house?" Jesus asked His mother. (Luke 2:49)

How do you parent the Son of God? How do you mother the God-Man when He is still a boy? I can't imagine the things she grappled with.

But I have felt just a sliver of her panic that Jesus might be gone. My heart has dropped as Mary's must have in the moment that she realized Jesus was not with the other boys. He was not with them. He was not with *her.*

Now, don't hear me wrong. I know that God is everywhere. I know that those who have called upon the saving name of Christ are filled with the Spirit of God – that He indwells us and will not abandon us (1 Corinthians 3:16; 2 Corinthians 1:21-22). I know that He will never leave us nor forsake us (Hebrews 13:15).

But I also know that it sometimes feels like He has.

Sometimes you lie in bed at night and wonder if the Lord whose presence you once knew has gone. You squeeze your eyes shut and beg to hear His voice the way you once did, the way that others say they have, but all you hear is the steady drum of your own heart. You put your face to the ground and beg for His intervention. I know that sometimes it doesn't seem to come.

He is always near. He is sometimes so very hard to find.

This was what I learned most during a season of life laced with disappointment. I wondered if I'd done something to warrant His withdrawal. I fought for the faith to trust He hadn't lost me. I searched through silence, church services, small groups, His Word, others' words. I clung to the truth even when it felt like my faith had been carved hollow and my hope had been drained.

I made coffee and did laundry. I wrote papers and took out the trash. I spent days whispering, "I know You're here," when it felt like the furthest thing from the truth. I stared at circumstances I didn't understand and pitched a few fits in the midst of them: "I don't understand *this.* I don't even understand *You.*" But I always ended up in the desperate, exhausted confession of "I still love You. And, oh, how I miss You."

I don't know when it happened. It wasn't a moment like when Mary found Jesus in the Temple. But slowly, over weeks and months, I began to feel the contented peace of His presence. I began to hear that still small voice I recognize as His.

Let's be clear. I'm not living in some beautiful, perfect place where I always feel His nearness and always hear Him clearly. There are still days of quiet. There are still many moments when I feel like I'm fumbling blind through a world that I can't quite figure out. A lot of my questions are still unresolved. I still don't understand why He's done some of the things He's done and allowed some of the things He's allowed in my life or in some of yours.

But there is this strange part of me that is grateful for it. For all of it – for every hard day, every confusing moment, every time I fought to cling to the one I couldn't see. Because it convinced me that what I want, more than anything, is to be *with* Him. I don't want to settle for being *about* Him. I don't want to pacify myself with being *for* Him. I don't just want to be *on* His side or *around* His people. I want to be *with Him*.

With Him. That is what I want to be.

Even when it doesn't look the way I expected. Even when it's hard, boring, or awkward. Even when it means confessing to the throngs of people that I'd lost Him for a moment, that I couldn't find Him, that I thought He might have gone. I want to be with Him because I love the face of the God-Man who looks up with that half smile when I find Him again. The one who says, *did you not know I was here?* The one I want to hug and hold and also pummel because He knew I couldn't find Him, because He's the one who allowed the search.

Furious relief.

Yes, I knew You were here, Lord. I knew You were good. I knew You were for me. I knew you were working on my behalf. But I couldn't find You.

And I didn't know how badly I needed to know You were with me.

I didn't know how desperate I was to be with You.

But now? Oh, now I do.

Respond

1. When (if ever) have you struggled to sense the Lord's presence or trust that He is there? What circumstances in your life or others' lives make you wonder where God is or what He is doing? What do you struggle to understand? When you struggle to understand God, are you likely to seek Him more or avoid Him? Take some time to be honest with yourself and your God about this.

2. What do you understand as the difference between being "about" or "for" Him and being "with" Him? Which most closely defines your relationship with Jesus right now?

While we won't always feel close to the Lord, we can intentionally position ourselves to remind ourselves of the Spirit's nearness even when He doesn't come to us in the way we expected.

Begin to pay attention to moments that seem to obstruct your view of the Lord. Are there things (even if they aren't bad things) that are taking up too much of your time or energy and distracting you from the Lord? Is there any activity or part of your routine that needs to be amended? Are there activities or habits that you should either put down or pick up in order to seek and see the Lord more clearly?

Ask Him to lay those things on your heart and to make you willing to obey. Try it this week! Don't be impulsive but also don't be afraid to experiment. Try quitting what you find distracting. Set down what turns your attention from the Lord. Pick up what you sense might help you seek Him. Then, pay attention. Did it make a difference? Discerning God's presence will take discipline and practice, but it will be so very worth it!

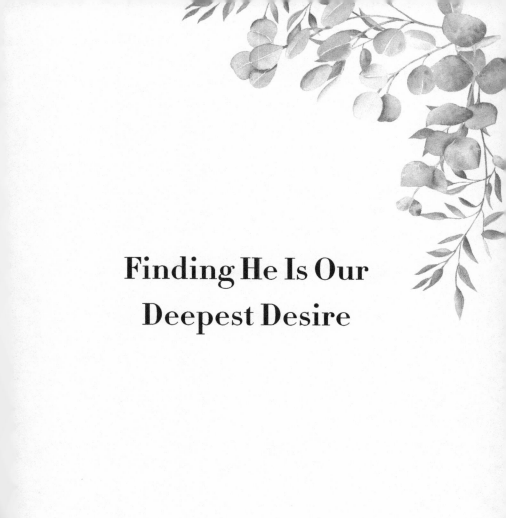

Finding He Is Our Deepest Desire

Surrender

The Woman with the Alabaster Jar
Luke 7:37-50

I sat with a book balanced on my legs, chicken salad and a bottle of water in a cooler next to my folding chair. I had braved a dip in the less-than-scenic Gulf waters to escape the Texas summer heat. I had come with my trusted dog to the beach for the day. I was escaping. Or exploring. Or just bored. It's hard to remember now. It also doesn't seem to matter. I know I was scared of a change I sensed was coming. I also know the change I anticipated never came. But other changes, unforeseen changes, would be upon me in a matter of weeks, and I think the Lord knew I needed to let go of a few things I'd been holding too tightly in order to receive what He would eventually give.

Seagulls squawked at their hunt through the seaweed. Children shrieked and splashed. Two teenagers threw a football – their bodies awkwardly formed but not yet filled. A man dunked his wife into the water. All the while, the waves crashed relentlessly against the shore. And I thought about how, even in the midst of all that chaos, God still saw a heart that had come to the shoreline

to remember how small I am, to glimpse how big He is, to find
room again to breathe – perhaps even to dance.

My mind wandered to the woman with the alabaster jar, the
one who brought her treasure to pour out on the feet of Christ:

> And there was a woman in the city who was a sinner;
> and when she learned that He was reclining at the
> table in the Pharisee's house, she brought an alabaster
> vial of perfume, and standing behind Him at His feet,
> weeping, she began to wet His feet with her tears, and
> kept wiping them with the hair of her head, and kissing
> His feet and anointing them with the perfume. (Luke
> 7:37-38)

She had always seemed to me so devoted, so reverent, so *holy*.
But that day at the beach, I let humanity crawl into her skin. I
let life lie in her bones. I let emotion swim in her tears. And I
wondered. Why did she cry? I let her past, her hopes, her fears,
and her failures cry out in need of a Savior. And I wondered if
we might not be so different. I let her hesitate and mourn. I let
her kneel in the presence of God Himself, and a little of her
own holiness waned as I let her sense the holiness of her God.

Did she kneel at His feet to remember how small she was? Did
His road-worn soles do for her what I came hoping this expanse
of ocean would do for me? Did she approach with her treasure in
hopes that she would remember He was worthy of it?

She wet His feet with her tears before breaking the ointment
jar over them. She wept in His presence before she poured
out her prize. I wonder about those tears. Perhaps as she knelt
there before her God, she cried because she wavered. Because

she hesitated. Because although she knew that He was worthy, she still counted the cost. I wonder if she grieved the loss of her treasure even as she chose to pour it out. I wonder if she wept before Him because she warred within herself – to keep what was rightly hers or to pour it out upon the one who had proven Himself so worthy of it.

I had always imagined her breaking that alabaster jar in confident worship. I wonder now if she did it more as some kind of desperate surrender – the ripping-off of a Band-Aid, the eyes-shut-tight leap from a ropes course, the dunk-your-head-beneath-the-waves commitment to a swim.

I have no way of knowing. Perhaps she was much braver than I am, but I suspect she was just as human. And even if she wasn't scared, I grasp at the hope-preserving possibility that she *could have* been. I grasp at the prospect that the Savior before whom she knelt is big enough to look at our trembling hands and still see the worship that we long to bring. I grasp at the promise that His strength is perfect in our weakness.

And I hold up my hands as if to show Him just how weak they really are. Not strong enough to hoard my treasure. Not strong enough to release it either.

Long after the gulls have flown on, the children have gone home, the husband and wife have left the water, the football toss has ended, and I have left the shore, the waves continue crashing. The monotonous rumbling testifies to the surety of our God. He is unwavering. He is undeterred. He is unmoved. He is no less God. No less worthy or holy. He is unthreatened by my hesitation.

He whispers a promise: "You have nothing to prove." And I find in His confidence the room to breathe. I try to whisper back that I trust Him, but He counters that I really don't.

And I admit that He's right. But I do *want* to trust Him.

And then I see it – the tiniest crack in the jar that holds what is most precious to me. I am both relieved and afraid, desiring to let go but tempted to continue to hoard, to find a new jar to catch my treasure.

And then He shows me, so tenderly, my two options: to watch the ointment leak, wasted onto the sand, or to pour it out on His feet. To waste what I have tried to save or to worship the one who offers life. And I exhale and weep as I break it open over His feet. But I breathe deeper, too, because it was never really mine. It was really, really heavy, and I was weary with the hoarding.

Sometimes we weep as ones torn by the worship of surrender but relieved by it too.

Jesus, with the fragrance of her offering still wet upon his feet, looked at the woman, "and He said to [her], 'Your faith has saved you; go in peace'" (Luke 7:50). I bet she could breathe again. I bet she could dance.

No, she hadn't come with anything to prove. And neither have I. And neither have you. We have come only with what we have been given. We walk in peace only when we give it back.

Kneeling small before our great big God, before the one who could choose to snatch the jar from our hand, we instead find one who basks in the fragrance of our offering. We find one who sees the struggle and rejoices in the gift. We find one who knew all along that we had to pour out our tears along with our treasures to receive His peace.

Emptied for the filling.

Yes, Lord, emptied. Be all that fills.

Respond

1. Why do you think remembering how big the Lord is and recognizing Him for who He is brings freedom? How have you experienced that in your own life?
2. What is it that you are afraid to surrender to the Lord? Do you cling to a relationship or circumstance or a dream? Is there anything in your life that you think you couldn't live without? Do you, like me, cling tightly to something to maintain some illusion of control? What treasure would you store in your alabaster jar?

Where do you best sense your smallness and the Lord's majesty? Either go there or picture yourself there, and worship the one who has proven Himself worthy. Let yourself sense the freedom that comes from giving God His rightful place of honor.

What treasure are you tempted to keep for yourself? What would it look like to pour it out on the feet of the one who will welcome your worship, accept your treasure, and value your presence? Worship the Lord with your surrender of all that you're tempted to hoard.

The Whole Truth

The Bleeding Woman

Mark 5:21-34

She ducked as she slipped through the crowd. An elbow grazed her ear. A man stepped back and knocked her forward. A child's foot danced over hers, but nothing deterred her. In fact, the opportunity for anonymity spurred her on. By Jewish law and societal pressures, this woman's condition forced her to live an isolated life. Physical contact with her would render another ceremonially unclean. Those around her had learned to keep their distance, and she had learned to stay away.

What holds us back from approaching our Healer?

In their excited frenzy, this crowd of people surrounding Christ provided the cover she needed to approach the Man who embodied her only remaining hope.

When Jesus was finally close enough to touch, she reached out boldly for the hem of His robe.

What do we know of this woman's isolation and imposed social distance that we didn't understand pre-pandemic? In a world where six feet was too close and staying away became a source of security, how grateful have we become that our physical or spiritual diseases do not threaten our Healer's wellness?

Instead of our illness making Him ill, His wellness somehow makes us well.

"Immediately the flow of blood dried up, and she felt in her body that she was healed of her disease" (Mark 5:29). Amazement soon gave way to uncertain anxiety as Jesus turned toward the crowd, "Who touched My garments?"

I imagine at this point that the woman faced a dilemma. She had already sensed her healing. She could have remained anonymous. Even Jesus' disciples inadvertently offered her a way out, explaining to Jesus that there was no way to know who touched Him: a whole crowd was reaching toward and jostling the Lord.

Jesus was focused, though. He was unhurried. Jesus continued looking through the throngs of people for the one who had touched Him. He had felt that power had left Him, and He wanted to know to whom it had gone.

Her body was healed, but Jesus also had in mind the things of the heart.

"The woman," the Scripture reads, "knowing what had happened to her, came in fear and trembling and fell down before Him and told Him the whole truth." (Mark 5:33)

She told Him the whole truth. I love that. Haven't we all done that? A question or a comment or a well-timed look sparks something in us. There is sometimes a brief moment where silence is still an option. But then, not sure where to begin or where to end, words pour from our lips and splash all over another. There might be tears or nervous laughter. There might be an awkward moment when we realize we've just "told the whole truth" regardless of whether they were really asking to hear it. We wait and pray and hope that either they will respond or we will disappear.

I don't have some big secret that I'm keeping from the Lord. I'm not withholding something that might shock Him – or even *you* for that matter. But some thoughts are brimming just below the surface, and I've spent too much time measuring words that I should have just gone ahead and said. It's a hard habit to break.

We find ourselves in a time when our minds are reeling from an overload of information and an absence of clarity.

We have to pause. We must release these jumbled thoughts and whirling what-ifs, opening our hearts and mouths, pouring our words out before a God who turns to His daughter and wants the "whole truth."

There is a quote I still remember from a journal I had in the sixth grade:

> Oh, the comfort, the inexpressible comfort of feeling safe with a person; having neither to weigh thoughts nor measure words, but to pour them all out, just as they are, chaff and grain together, knowing that a faithful hand will take and sift them, keep what is worth keeping, and then, with a breath of kindness, blow the rest away.[4]

Yes, such comfort. Several years ago, I told a newer friend a detail of my story that I don't tell many people. It isn't even scandalous, but it involves a few too many people to share openly. You know the kind. We all have them. After recounting the story to her, she said, "Oh, yeah, I had already figured that out." *Oh. Well, then. Good.*

---

4 Mulock, Dinah Marie. A Life for a Life. New York: Carleton, 1866.

Sometimes our secrets tell on us before we tell them. But there is such freedom in speaking them in the right place, to the right people, at the right time.

Like that friend who had already figured it out but waited for me to decide to share, our God looks at our hearts and lets the unspoken things remain until we are ready to give them a voice.

He knows. But He waits.

He stands in the middle of a bustling crowd and asks who has reached for Him. And we stand, longing to fall before Him but terrified of it too. We long to step out and be seen, but we are terrified of being exposed.

Until the pressure builds in our chest, and the fear of being passed by is greater than the fear of being known.

And we lay before Him, and the words fall out choppy and unmeasured. And we stop trying to make sense of it, and we just tell Him what we know, what we saw, what has happened.

And it doesn't feel at all holy, but we know it somehow is.

There she lay, on the ground before the Lord in front of a mass of people, wondering what He might say. Would He be angry that she had touched Him? Would He be appalled by her? Ashamed of her? Would He be annoyed by the delay? Would others laugh? Would she care? Would He revoke the healing? Could He?

There is safety in anonymity, and I'd have understood it if she'd chosen to slip away.

But then His response: "Daughter, your faith has healed you." (Mark 5:34). He called her *daughter*.

I don't know why some people are healed physically this side of heaven and some aren't. I don't know why some healing is immediate, and some takes time. But I do know that I would rather engage my Healer than quietly nurse my wounds. I would rather reach out for His cloak with my last bit of faith and hope than stand silent in a crowd and assume He wouldn't move to heal me. I'm pretty sure that whether the bleeding stops, I'd rather be clinging to the hem of Christ's robe than releasing hope altogether.

Tell Him the whole truth, daughter. Because He is a Father who is faithful to comfort, to heal, to cover.

He already knows, but He longs to hear. Because He knows there is healing in the telling.

Respond

1. What holds you back from approaching the Lord? Please take some time to consider this. What are you afraid might happen? What are you afraid might not happen? Allow yourself to be still and consider this. Be honest about it.
2. Can you think of a time when you released a secret and found healing and freedom as you did?

Take some time now in the presence of our Lord to "tell Him the whole truth." Tell Him how badly it hurts, how it feels when no one else understands, how much courage it took to push through the throng of people and reach for His robe. Tell Him how excited you were when you first sensed your healing. Tell Him how disappointed you were when the healing seemed to fail. Tell Him what you're afraid of. Tell Him everything. Open your mouth and begin to speak. Talk until you're finished. Even with everything else going on in the world, He has all the time you need.

Letting Go
Mary Magdalene at the Tomb
John 20:1-18

Every year at Easter, I am struck by the exchange between Jesus and Mary Magdalene outside the empty tomb. It is Jesus' words to Mary: "Do not cling to Me" (John 20:17).

Did Jesus really say that?

I can almost feel His strong hands gently prying His robe from her fists. Why couldn't she hold on? She had come broken and grieving. Confusion and despair descended when Jesus was not there. But then her heart had rejoiced to hear Him speak her name. Her spirit leapt when she realized He had risen. Her hands reached. And they clung. I can understand why.

But then He made her let go. My heart aches for her at the thought of it.

Why? I ask Him as though it were my own hands clutching His robe. And then another verse of Scripture echoes in my mind: "Remember Lot's wife" (Luke 17:32).

I'm sorry, I want to say, *I do not understand what You are talking about.* But I do. He is talking, I think, about hearts that cling to the way things *were* while He is moving us forward. He is talking about our longing for familiarity at the expense of His will. He is talking about clutching what we've always known when He has something much better in mind.

As God ushered Lot and his family from Sodom and Gomorrah, sparing them from the judgment He poured out on those cities, Lot's wife looked back. She longed for some strangely idealized memory of what had been. She ached for what once was and feared what was to come.

And so, before Jesus' death, when He spoke of His coming kingdom and His future return, He reminded them of Lot's wife.

Perhaps so they wouldn't try to walk forward with their eyes fixed on the past.

Will we miss the Coming King because we hold too tightly to the world we've known? Will we cling to our kingdoms and miss the one He's ushering in? Will we try to back our way into the future that Christ has prepared for us?

My heart breaks for Mary because I am a clinger. I want to hold on. I want to clutch the things I've known. I will white-knuckle "the way it's been" as though I might convince God to let me stay. Or perhaps I have my feet planted firmly in the familiar, and I'm clinging onto Him in hopes that *He'll* stay. I think maybe that's what Mary was doing. Maybe she was holding onto the Jesus she'd always known, to the way that He had always been, when He was doing something new. He had risen from the dead after all! Things would never be the same. But that didn't keep her heart from longing for familiar. It didn't keep her hands from reaching for the one she'd known.

Mary, feet planted by the empty tomb, clung to the Lord, silently begging Him to stay right there. He was on His way to the Father, though. He would send the Holy Spirit. He would establish the church. He would roll out the kingdom of God onto this fragile sod. He would – He *will* – one day return in glory and power. Without realizing it, Mary held onto the way it had been and risked missing His greater glory.

But she didn't miss it, and I don't want to either.

I look down at my white knuckles. Am I clinging to Jesus in a way that begs Him not to move? Am I hesitant to let Him lead me into the new? Instead, I am tempted to cling to the way it's always been while He whispers a promise that it will be better, even if it's hard.

I am clinging to a life with which I am familiar, and He is beckoning me to lay it down.

For just a moment, I'm frozen right there with Mary, and Jesus has just spoken words I never thought I'd hear: "Do not cling to Me." And I want to ask Mary if it was worth it. Do we let go? Do we lay this down? Do we actually leave this here? Even though it hurts? Even though it's scary? Even though we don't know what's coming? Do we let Him go so that He can lead?

Mary, did He really ask you to let go? How did you summon the strength to obey?

Instead of her reply, I hear the voice of her Lord: "I give them eternal life, and they will never perish, and no one will snatch them out of my hand. My Father, who has given them to me, is greater than all, and no one is able to snatch them out of the Father's hand" (John 10:28-29). My death grip loosens, and I realize I've been holding my breath.

Sometimes He has to pry things out of our hands to show us how tightly He holds us in His.

Respond

1. Mary sought Jesus in a place where He no longer was. Circumstances had changed. He was still present, and He would continue to be present by the pouring out of His Spirit, but it would be different. She needed to learn to see Him with different eyes. Where have you been looking to find Jesus in your daily life but failing to see Him? Are there places or ways you have seen Him before that you no longer sense Him in this season? Might He be inviting you to see Him in new or different ways as your circumstances change? Ask Him to give you eyes and faith to see Him and recognize Him as He meets you in *these* days.

2. In times of transition, are you usually tempted to look back in a way that holds you back? What circumstances in your life have recently changed, or where do you sense a change is coming? Are you hesitant to walk forward with the Lord into a new season? Why? What will you miss about the season that you have been in? Engage the Lord in any season of change. He can give us the courage to walk confidently forward *with* Him.

The discipline of fasting trains our hands and hearts to release the things of this world that Jesus asks us to release. We don't fast to prove anything to God or to manipulate Him. We don't fast to earn or secure His favor. We fast to turn our eyes to Jesus — to the one who was crucified, died, and was buried. The one who rose again and encountered Mary at the tomb, the one who returned to the Father and now sits in the place of honor and glory. What is something you could fast from and "release" this week? Use its absence and the gaps it leaves to intentionally turn your eyes to Jesus and ask Him to reveal a new and different facet of Himself this week as you do.

Arise

Jairus' Daughter

Mark 5:21-43

Writing these devotionals has been the best kind of hard. It has driven me to the Scriptures with the kind of determination that I might have missed if I'd been left on my own. I read better when I'm writing. I listen better and think better. I think *more*. I lean my head over the pages of God's Word with an intensity that is both exhausting and exhilarating. I feel so much more alive.

We were created to actually live, you know. Yet, we settle for so much less.

Jairus' little girl's grip on life was loosening. He'd sat beside her bed and watched her laughter slip to lethargy. He'd watched the fog of fever gloss over her once-animated eyes. He'd watched as weariness pulled her inside of herself, and the color drained from her cheeks as clammy hands curled into fists to fight the pain. He'd watched her fight run out and give way to restless sleep. He'd watched those fists unfurl the way they had when life was new, and sleep was welcomed. He'd watched the life drip from her delicate fingertips. And he'd run to drop himself at the feet of Christ.

Thank God for fathers who will not stand idly by as death smothers their daughters. (If you didn't have a father who would hunt down healing on your behalf, rest assured you have a Father in Heaven who will!)

There is much to be said about the heart of Jairus – this father who sought the Healer with courage that only desperation allows. But I want to focus more on the little girl because I would wager that most of us are more comfortable seeking the Healer for another than waiting lifelessly for a miracle of our own.

Has your vibrant laughter faded to a jaded smile? Do your eyes blink heavily against the fog? When did weariness convince you to withdraw? What drained the life blood from your face? Why did your hands curl into fists itching for a fight with a world that does not fight fair? When did that fight give way to exhausted acceptance of what you were never meant to bear? What has worn you down and laid you out? How has death slipped silently into a place intended for so much life?

Once news came that the little girl had died, Jesus was selective about those He invited to accompany Him to her side. He took three of His closest disciples and the little girl's parents. Anticipating the miracle, Jesus protected this daughter from the uncomfortable stares of curious onlookers. When the room emptied of wailing mourners and filled with hesitant hope, the Lord reached for the child's hand and spoke directly to her: "Little girl, I say to you, arise" (Mark 5:41). And immediately, we're told, she "got up and began walking" (Mark 5:42).

Our God comes in such tender power. He is the Father who does not stand idly by.

Sometimes He works in strange ways. Sometimes He allows our numb hearts to feel the depth of the pain again before He comes to heal. Sometimes He allows the shame to nearly smother us before He lifts it off and sets us free. Sometimes, as He did in this little girl's story, He allows our ailing selves to die before He calls us back to life. I don't really know why He does that, but maybe it's to ensure we don't miss the miracle.

Like most of you, I have been through several seasons in the quiet place where it's just Jesus and a couple of others. I have spent a lot of time with my hand tucked safely in His, learning to walk again on legs that are weak but sturdy. I'm so grateful for this life, but I fear I may have grown reluctant to really *live* it. Doesn't He know it's dangerous? Doesn't He know that these people have germs (literally and figuratively)? They stare at me. They ask questions that they have not earned the answer to. They flippantly say and do things that cut deeper than they intend. They share opinions I didn't ask to know. *This life can kill you, You know, Lord.*

And He gently pulls His hand from mine so that I might see the scars. *Yes, I do know,* His eyes remind me.

Jesus gave this little girl miraculous life. Fresh breath filled her lungs. A once-stilled heart beat again, warming her hands and flushing her cheeks. But even with that new life, she could have stayed in bed for fear the fever might return. She could have sat up slowly, cautiously, knowing now the perils of life in this world. And so can we. We can protect ourselves right out of our healing and worry ourselves right back into our shame. We can miss our whole lives for fear of death. But we don't have to!

The Risen One beckons us *arise*, and He takes our hand as He calls us forth. We do not go alone. We go with the God who has given us new life and who binds up our wounds. We go with the God who bears our burdens and forgives our sins. We walk in the wisdom and power of His Spirit. And in His abundant provision, we go with each other – the body of Christ filled with the very Spirit of Christ. And we find that even with all their germs and stares and differing opinions, we still want very much to be a part of them. It is *safer* to exist without them, but it isn't really *living* at all.

I love the ending of this story. Before He departed the little girl's house, Jesus "told them to give her something to eat" (Mark 5:43). I guess if you've been so sick that you've died and then been raised from the dead, you have probably worked up an appetite. You are probably famished. And you might be so grateful for life that you forget the fundamentals of living – like eating.

You might forget to do the very things that sustain the life that Christ has restored.

He intends for us to *live* this life He's given. He intends for us to do those things that give us life and remind us of how much we love it. For me, it is writing, reading, and long walks with friends who will listen to all of my words and sift through them for meaning. It's ice cream with my mom and painting furniture and rocking babies.

It's relaxing against the reality of the Father, who insisted upon the healing that would lead to life. And then insisted that I actually live that life.

When I would have settled for so much less.

Respond

1. Search your heart. Where has lethargy or complacency or despair produced a death where God intends there to be life?
2. What does it look like in your own life to "protect yourself from living"? What actions (or inactions) are you prone to when trying to avoid taking risks or being vulnerable? If we can recognize the patterns we turn to, we can more quickly turn to Jesus when we recognize ourselves falling back to our old, self-protective ways. Write down God's promise in Psalm 3:3 and put it somewhere to remind you of the one whose job is to protect you.

What activities make you feel the most alive? (Don't worry about making them sound "spiritual". If they aren't sinful, they're fair game for this question.) Schedule one of those activities into your week, and invite Jesus into it. Arise. Live! Enjoy Him and His presence as you enjoy something He created you to love doing.

As you go forward from here, continue to make time to do the things with the Lord that sustain the life that God has restored!

By Jesus' Side

The Women of Luke 8

Luke 8:1-3

As Christ walked through the cities and villages, "proclaiming and bringing the good news of the kingdom of God" (Luke 8:1), His twelve disciples were with Him, "and also some women who had been healed of evil spirits and infirmities: Mary, called Magdalene, from whom seven demons had gone out, and Joanna, the wife of Chuza, Herod's household manager, and Susanna, and many others, who provided for them out of their means" (Luke 8:2-3).

The women who walked with Jesus provided for Jesus and His followers. They gave what they had to offer, and they gave it freely. But they did it as they walked beside Him. They did it as their hearts were stirred by His presence and His goodness. They did it because they looked and found Him worthy.

I used to keep an index card next to my computer. It said this: "All the women whose hearts stirred them to use their skill spun the goats' hair" (Exodus 35:26).

Doesn't that leave you inspired?

Perhaps not. But give it a chance because, in its context, it does something in my heart.

The people of Israel had been delivered from slavery in Egypt by miraculous signs and wonders. They had crossed the Red Sea on dry land to escape death at the hands of the Pharoah. The Lord Himself led them in a pillar of cloud by day and a pillar of fire by night. He had called Moses up to Mount Sinai and had delivered the Law to Israel, which sounds burdensome but was actually a beautiful invitation to live before Him, the holy and magnificent God who pledged Himself to be *their* God. Included in that law were instructions for building a Tabernacle.

The purpose of that Tabernacle?

"And let them make Me a sanctuary, that I may dwell in their midst." (Exodus 25:8)

That God Himself might dwell among them!

It was a tent made of the people's earthly possessions according to the Lord's instruction by the people's strength and skill. The Lord gave the order (Exodus 35:4). The people gave willingly:

> Everyone whose heart was moved and whose spirit prompted him came and brought an offering to the Lord for the work on the tent of meeting, for all its services, and for the holy garments. Both men and women came; all who had willing hearts brought brooches, earrings, rings, necklaces, and all kinds of jewelry – everyone who presented a presentation offering to the Lord... Every skilled woman spun yarn with her hands and brought it...And all the women who were moved spun the goat hair by virtue of her skill...So the Israelites brought a freewill offering to the Lord. (Exodus 35:21-29, *excerpts,* CSB)

All the women whose hearts stirred them to use their skill. They brought a freewill offering to the Lord.

The people brought what He desired. The people brought what they had. Until Moses had to tell them to stop because they had brought more than enough (Exodus 36:5). Oh, might that be said of us? That we brought what we had? That we gave it willingly? That we gave until there was more than enough?

Might we be women whose hearts stir us to share our skills?

Inside the Tabernacle complex was a bronze basin, which was used for purification (Exodus 30:18-21). The bronze basin was made from the mirrors of the ministering women – the mirrors they had given freely: "He made the basin of bronze and its stand of bronze, from the mirrors of the ministering women who ministered at the tent of meeting" (Exodus 38:8).

Some women spun the goats' hair. Some women gave their mirrors. All contributed to the dwelling place of the Lord who desired to dwell among them (Exodus 25:8).

The women who lived in the time of Christ? They did the same; they walked beside the Christ who had come to dwell in their midst. The same God who had set His glory in the Tabernacle wrapped Himself in flesh and dwelt among His people. As Christ walked through the cities and villages, "proclaiming and bringing the good news of the kingdom of God" (Luke 8:1), His twelve disciples were with Him, as were those women who walked beside Him.

The healed. The wives. The managers. The providers. The grateful.

May we be counted among them. The God who walked among them still dwells within our midst, still walks faithfully beside us today. That very same God has set His Spirit within all who call upon the saving name of Christ.

Some women raise their babies. Some raise others' babies. Some file papers. Some speak. Some minister inside the church. Some minister outside of it. Some write books. Some serve their neighbors in mansions. Some serve the poor in forgotten corners of the world. Some bathe those who can no longer bathe themselves. Some heal and serve and give life to their husbands with words and touches that no one else will ever see. Some intercede on their knees for people whose thanks they will not know this side of heaven. Some serve communion. Some serve coffee. Some lead movements. Some lead boardrooms. Some lead classrooms. Some lead homes.

May we serve the way our hearts stir, the way our circumstances direct, and the way our resources allow.

May we give what we have with cheerful hearts: Our time. Our love. Our money. Our lives.

May we melt our mirrors into basins that others might wash in the love of Christ.

May we spin our goats' hair into a dwelling place for God.

May we bring what we have. May we bring it gladly. May we see His glory.

May we walk beside Christ, filled by the Spirit of Christ, shoulder-to-shoulder with women who do the same.

May we live longing and looking for the presence of the Lord who still chooses to dwell right here in our midst.

Respond

1. What does it mean to you that the same presence of God whose glory dwelt in the Tabernacle, who took on flesh and walked among the women of ancient times, dwells within you by His Spirit today? What does that teach you about His nearness? What does that teach you about the power that resides within you by the Holy Spirit? (Consider Romans 8:11 for further reflection.)

2. When have you experienced the presence of the Lord as you served Him by serving or giving to others? Have you sensed His joy or His approval? We don't serve to gain acceptance from Him, but His acceptance and movement in our lives often stirs us to serve!

Sometimes we need a really practical application. I'm asking the Lord to speak clearly to you as you consider how He might be inviting you to serve. The women who walked with Jesus "provided for Him out of their means" (Luke 8:3). They gave what they had to offer, and they gave it freely. But they did it as they walked beside Him. They did it as His presence and goodness stirred their hearts. They did it because they looked and found Him worthy.

When you consider the nearness of Christ and the power of His Spirit within you, what are you stirred to bring to Him? Perhaps it is some act of service or some material possession? What do you long to do for or give to the Lord? Try serving that way this week, but as you do, actively involve the Lord in your service or giving. Invite Him into every moment. Acknowledge His presence in every move. He doesn't need our service, but He graciously invites us to partner with Him, and when we do, we get to walk by His side and provide with Him from the very things and skills He has first given to us.

Acknowledgements

The Lord has used these ancient women of the Gospels to reveal Himself to me, but He has also used the women who walk by my side. These women have pushed me closer to Lord. They have shown me His character. They have been His arms wrapped tight around me. They have been His voice, speaking encouragement and love. They have been His hands, steadying me each step of the way.

"Thank you" will never be sufficient, but it will have to be enough.

Thank you, Mom, for being my first audience. From preschool scribble to middle school essays to my first attempts at Bible study to today. You have never hesitated to push me to make it "better," and that has made me confident to know that I *could* make it better. You are the person I trust the most with my words.

Thank you, Kathy Phillips, for teaching me how to study the Bible and for reminding me that it's never just for the sake of knowledge. You taught me what it means to seek the Presence of God, and you have made me satisfied with nothing less. You believed I could write Bible studies before I had thought to try, and that has given me the courage to do it.

Thank you, Lindsee Eddy, for listening to my stream of conscious ramblings about this project, for reading and re-reading sentences that were barely changed, and for being brave enough to argue with me. As my roommate, you have seen the very worst things about me, and you still choose to be my friend. I'm grateful.

Thank you, Katie Lock, for learning with me that walks could be prayers. Jesus was right by our side all those days, and you continue to point me to Him. Thank you for your never-failing confidence that this book would be written.

Thank you, Corlischa Badenhorst, for figuring out the world of "women's ministry" with me. Thank you for letting me fail and fumble and for continuing to trust me. I'm grateful for your friendship!

Thank you, Morgan Roberts, for seeking Jesus alongside me since the awkward days of high school. Thank you for "showing up" and teaching me the power of being present.

Thank you, Granny, for the perfect picture of what unrestrained love and delight feels like. You have been overly impressed with me for my entire life, which you've said is your right as a grandmother. I can't complain! You have many times revealed to me what the love of God is like.

Thank you to three women who travelled to Israel with me as strangers and returned as friends. Julie, Lisa, and Tiffany, you have known me through every season of my adulthood. You have graciously allowed me to grow up around you without ever making me feel insignificant. You'll never know what a gift it is to me.

Thank you to my Monday Night Small Group for being willing to try every Bible study idea I have. I love seeking God with you. I know Him better because of you.

And, in breaking with the theme of women, thank you to four men who have given me the courage and resources to pursue this dream of writing a book.

Thank you, Curtis Jones, for telling me to "go for it" when I said I wanted to teach. Thank you for opening up opportunities for me to do that. Your encouragement has done exactly what encouragement should: it has given me the courage to keep going!

Thank you, Grandaddy Dub, for believing I am capable of almost anything. Your sacrifices and generosity make it possible for me to do what I love doing.

Thank you, Dad, for making me laugh. I'm thankful for your sarcasm and your wit. You remind me not to take myself (or anyone else) too seriously. You've kept my feet planted firmly on the soil of earth when I might have drifted off into a theoretical, theological cloud. I trust the love of the Father easily because of your love for me.

And thank you, to the Man of Christ for the gift of your Spirit and the assurance of your presence. You stand right by my side, even when I forget that You are there. No one has tended to me as You have.

Other Resources from Cody

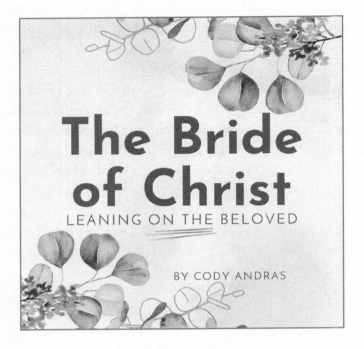

The Bride of Christ: Leaning on the Beloved

In this eight week study, Cody leads you on a journey through Scripture to explore what it means that we are called the bride of Christ and how to relate to Jesus as our Bridegroom.

The study invites you to:
- Recognize the significance of your identity as the bride of Christ
- Approach Jesus with confident trust that you are welcome In His Presence
- Rest In the love of God rather than wear yourself out trying to earn His love
- Depend on the faithful love and companionship of our Most High God

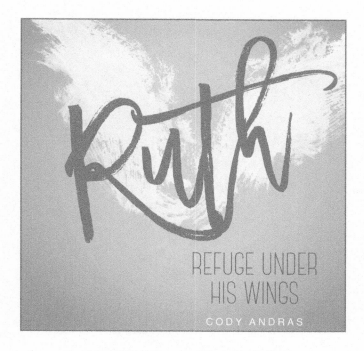

Ruth: Refuge Under His Wings

In this devotional, you will walk through the story of Ruth, considering what it teaches about the Lord's provision, protection, and restoration of us as His beloved.

Each of the six devotional lessons includes:

- A written teaching by Cody
- Three reflection questions
- A prayer prompt for your personal time with the Lord
- A personal testimony from a woman who living under the wings of the One True God today

"And when we wander, may we return to the Lord more quickly than before.

May we recognize His relief and rest even as we wait.

May we know we are redeemed.

May we seek to be restored."

A Place In His Presence: God's Eternal Plan to Draw Us to Himself

A Place in His Presence is a nine-week Bible study that looks at the whole story of Scripture.

The Lord's plan, revealed in Genesis through Revelation, has always been to draw His people back to Himself. This study follows the developments of that plan through the major events of Scripture.

Cody leads you through God's plans for His creation and guides you to consider your place in His story as you find your place in His Presence.

A Promised Hope: The Coming King

We tend to use the word "hope" as a synonym for "wish." But hope is meant to have a more securing hold than that. Hope is meant to steady us. Hope is meant to anchor us regardless of the seas we're tossed upon.

Find your footing in these most uncertain of times by:

- Reattaching the good news of what Christ has done on the cross with the good news of what He has promised to do when He returns
- Placing your hope in the constant faithfulness of the Lord
- Considering promises from the Old and New Testaments of what the Messiah will do when He returns
- Understanding what it means to live your life in light of the fact that our King is coming back

Made in the USA
Coppell, TX
26 June 2023

18539231R00088